I0361264

CHASING AURORA AUSTRALIS

ARUN CHANDRAN

First Edition

June 2024

Copyright © 2024 Arun Chandran

All rights reserved.

ChasingAurora.com.au

Cover photo taken by Arun Chandran.

No part of this book may be reproduced, stored in a retrieval system, or transmitted in any form or by any means, electronic, mechanical, photocopying, recording, or otherwise, without the prior written permission of the author, except in the case of brief quotations embodied in critical reviews and certain other non-commercial uses permitted by copyright law.

For permission requests, please write to the author at:

chasingauroraaustralis@gmail.com

ISBN: 9781763626614

DEDICATION

To my incredible wife, my partner in crime and the best navigator anyone could ask for – your unique sense of adventure adds a special spark to every trip we take together.

To my parents, the original adventurers, who taught me that the world is a whole of wonder and waiting to be explored.

To my brother and family, the best travel companions and cheerleaders, your unwavering support and infectious enthusiasm are the pillars that fuel my journeys.

And to my friends, your unwavering support and limitless encouragement have been the pillars of my journey, and I am forever grateful for your presence in my life.

Here's to all of you – let's keep the adventure going!

CHASING AURORA AUSTRALIS

CONTENTS

1	The Science Behind Aurora Australis	1
2	The Best Time to See Aurora Australis	7
3	Understanding Aurora Forecast Parameters	13
4	Aurora Apps, Websites, And Communities	24
5	Mastering The Skies With Cloud Cover Forecasts	41
6	Lights, Camera, Action!	47
7	The Epic Geomagnetic Storm Of May 2024	59
8	What Makes Aurora Hunting Very Addictive?	63
9	Aurora Hunting Needs A Lot Of Patience	67
10	STEVE	71
11	Prime Aurora Locations - NZ	73
12	Prime Aurora Locations - TAS	103
13	Prime Aurora Locations - VIC	139
14	Prime Aurora Locations - SA	193
15	Prime Aurora Locations - WA	207
16	Prime Aurora Locations - ACT	225
17	Prime Aurora Locations - NSW	227
18	FAQs On Aurora Australis	235
19	Space Weather Glossary	265

CHASING AURORA AUSTRALIS

1
THE SCIENCE BEHIND AURORA AUSTRALIS

The story of the Southern Lights (Aurora Australis) starts 150 million kilometres away from the Sun. Our Sun is a giant ball of hot gas that constantly bubbles and boils. Sometimes, it gets excited and throws a tantrum, sending vast bursts of energy and charged particles into space. This is called a solar wind, and during big tantrums, we get solar flares or coronal mass ejections (CMEs). Sunspots are dark spots on the Sun's surface that are cooler than the surrounding areas. They are associated with increased solar activity, including solar flares and coronal mass ejections (CMEs).

So, what exactly is solar wind? Think of it as the Sun's breath. Just like when you blow on a dandelion, and the seeds scatter everywhere, the Sun releases particles from its surface and scatters them throughout the solar system. These particles are primarily electrons and protons, travelling outwards and carrying energy.

Solar flares are like the Sun's version of fireworks. They happen when magnetic energy in the Sun's atmosphere gets released simultaneously. Satellites like the Solar Dynamics Observatory (SDO) closely watch the Sun. They capture images and data in X-ray and UV light, showing us the flare's intensity and size. The flare's brightness in these images tells scientists how powerful it is. They use a scale from A, B, C, M, to X, with A being the smallest and X being the biggest flares.

CMEs are like the Sun's confetti cannon blasts. They shoot out vast clouds of solar particles into space. Measuring these explosive events involves a few cool techniques:

1. Coronagraphs: These are special instruments on satellites that block out the Sun's bright light, like putting on sunglasses. This helps scientists see the faint CMEs as they travel through space.

2. Speed and Direction: Scientists can track the speed and direction of a CME by taking a series of images. This helps them predict if and when it might hit Earth.

3. Particle Detectors: Instruments on satellites also measure the particles and magnetic fields from CMEs when they reach Earth. This gives scientists more information about their strength and potential impact.

These charged particles race through space at incredible speeds, making their way toward Earth.

DSCOVR (short for Deep Space Climate Observatory) is a satellite that hangs out in space between the Earth and the Sun. Its job is to keep an eye on the solar wind. DSCOVR has special sensors that can detect and measure the particles in the solar wind. These sensors count the number of particles, measure their speed, and check their temperature. It's like a weather station in space, but it measures solar particles and energy instead of measuring rain and wind. DSCOVR also has a tool to measure the magnetic field carried by the solar wind.

But don't worry; our planet has a defence system: the magnetic field. Think of Earth's magnetic field as a giant bubble surrounding our planet. This bubble is created by the movement of molten iron in Earth's outer core. Like how stirring a soup pot makes swirls and currents, the swirling iron creates electric currents, producing the magnetic field. This magnetic field protects us from most of the Sun's charged particles.

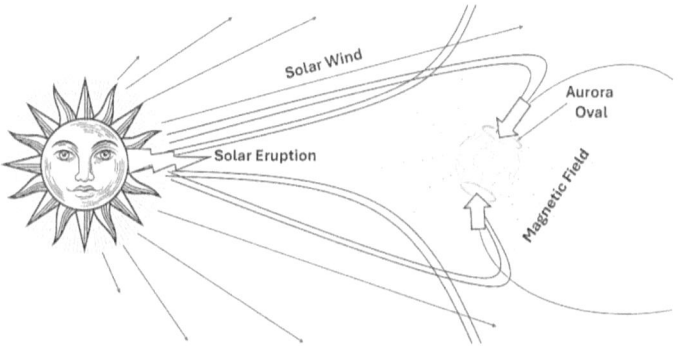

When the solar wind reaches Earth, here's what happens:

1. **Deflection:** The magnetic field deflects most solar wind particles like a superhero's shield deflects enemy attacks. This keeps the particles from hitting Earth directly and protects our atmosphere.

2. **Magnetosphere Distortion:** The solar wind squishes the magnetic field on the side facing the Sun and stretches it out on the opposite side, creating a long tail called the magnetotail. Earth's force field gets dented and stretched.

3. **Exciting the Atmosphere:** Some particles get trapped in the magnetic field and spiral toward the poles, colliding with atmospheric gases.

Now, here's where the magic happens. The charged particles collide with gases in the atmosphere, like oxygen and nitrogen. Imagine these gases as excited party-goers at a cosmic disco. When they get hit by the particles, they absorb energy and get excited, jumping to higher energy levels.

But party-goers can't stay excited forever. When the gases calm down and return to normal, they release that extra energy as light. The specific colours depend on the type of gas and the collision's altitude. Different gases give off different colours:

Oxygen - The Green and Red Artist

- Green: The most common colour in auroras is a bright, vivid green. This happens when oxygen molecules high up in the atmosphere (around 100 kilometres above Earth) get excited and emit light. Think of it as the Earth's way of showing off a flashy emerald dress!

- Red: When oxygen molecules even higher up (around 240 kilometres) get into the act, they glow red. This rare colour adds a splash of scarlet to the auroral palette, giving it a fiery, dramatic touch.

Nitrogen - The Blue and Purple Wizard

- Blue: Nitrogen is the magician responsible for the stunning blue shades. When nitrogen gets a jolt of energy, it can glow blue, adding a cool, mystical hue to the auroras. It's like the night sky is wearing sapphire jewellery!

- Purple/Violet: Sometimes, nitrogen molecules mix things up by emitting purple or violet light. These colours are less common but add a magical, otherworldly feel to the auroras, like a celestial sorcerer's spell.

Hydrogen and Helium - The Subtle Spectators

- Pink and Yellow: While oxygen and nitrogen steal the show, hydrogen and helium play a part, though they're more subtle. They can contribute to the pinks and yellows seen in auroras. Imagine these colours as the pastel highlights in the grand auroral painting.

These lights combine to create the stunning display we call the Aurora Australis. The lights usually appear as shimmering curtains, arcs, or even spirals of light dancing across the sky. The shape and movement of the auroras are influenced by the Earth's magnetic field and the intensity of the solar wind.

Astronauts aboard the International Space Station (ISS) often get front-row seats to this incredible light show. From their vantage point, they can see the auroras as glowing, colourful curtains of light dancing across the Earth's atmosphere. The view from space offers a unique perspective different from what we see on the ground.

Auroras aren't exclusive to Earth; they occur on other planets with magnetic fields and atmospheres.

Here's a quick tour of auroras in our solar system:

1. **Jupiter:** Jupiter's auroras are massive and incredibly powerful. They are caused by its strong magnetic field and the particles from its moon, Io, which is volcanically active. The result is an aurora that's a hundred times more powerful than Earth's!

2. **Saturn:** Saturn also puts on a beautiful aurora show. Its auroras are primarily in ultraviolet light, so they're not visible to the naked eye, but they are stunning when captured by unique cameras.

3. **Uranus and Neptune:** These ice giants have auroras too! Though not as well-studied as those on Jupiter and Saturn, the Hubble Space Telescope has captured images of faint auroras on Uranus and Neptune.

4. **Mars:** Mars has a weaker magnetic field compared to Earth, so its auroras are more localized and less intense. They are known as "discrete auroras" and can be found in specific regions of the Martian atmosphere. The solar storms that treated us to those jaw-dropping auroras on May 11th, 2024, didn't stop there. A month later, they turned their sights on Mars, whipping dazzling auroras over the Red Planet and blasting its surface with harmful radiation. The culprit behind these wild solar storms was AR3664, an intense, hyperactive region on the sun. This magnetic knot was packed with dozens of sunspots that fired off a barrage of powerful flares and coronal mass ejections (CMEs). First, they aimed right at Earth, and as the sun's rotation continued, they took direct aim at Mars. Talk about a cosmic one-two punch!

2
THE BEST TIME TO SEE AURORA AUSTRALIS

The Southern Lights can technically be seen at any time of the year. However, there are a few other factors to consider.

Solar Maximum: Between 2024 - 2026

Solar activity is cranking up the heat in Solar Cycle 25! The National Oceanic and Atmospheric Administration's (NOAA) Space Weather Prediction Center (SWPC) forecasts a spectacular solar maximum, expected to dazzle us between late 2024 and early 2026.

Solar maximum: This is the Sun's activity cycle peak, which happens about every 11 years. During a solar maximum, the Sun is super active. It sends out more solar flares and solar wind, which are streams of charged particles. When these particles hit Earth's magnetic field, they create stunning auroras. So, during solar maximum, you have a higher chance of seeing brighter and more frequent auroras lighting up the sky.

Solar Minimum: This is the opposite of solar maximum. It's the period when the Sun is at its quietest. There are fewer solar flares and less solar wind. As a result, auroras are less frequent and less intense. But don't worry! Even during a solar minimum, you can still catch some auroras. They might not be as strong or common as during a solar maximum.

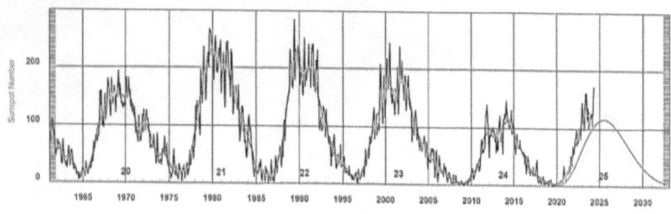

NOAA - Space Weather Prediction Center

Why Winter is the Best Season to See the Magical Aurora

Winter nights are longer and darker. The aurora needs a dark sky to shine its brightest, and in winter, the Sun sets early and rises late. This gives you more hours to catch the light show. Plus, with less daylight, there's less chance of light pollution spoiling the view.

Winter weather often brings clear skies. While it can be chilly, those cold, crisp nights are perfect for aurora watching. The air is often clearer in winter, and the stars and auroras are spectacularly visible when clouds do part.

Magical Time: 10 PM and 2 AM

The secret sauce to catching the Aurora Australis is the aurora oval. Between 10 PM and 2 AM, the aurora oval—the ring-shaped zone where auroras are most visible—perfectly aligns with your viewing location. This alignment makes the lights more intense and easier to spot.

Darkness is your best friend when hunting for auroras. The night is at its deepest and darkest between 10 PM and 2 AM. This deep darkness makes the vibrant colours of the aurora pop against the night sky, giving you a clearer and more spectacular view.

Late night to early morning usually means clearer skies. The hustle and bustle of daytime winds down, reducing atmospheric disturbances. Fewer clouds mean better conditions in which to enjoy the light show.

Equinoxes: March and September

An equinox happens twice a year, around March 21 and September 21. These are the days when day and night are almost equal in length. But what makes them unique for aurora viewing?

During the equinoxes, the Earth's magnetic field aligns just right with the solar wind. Think of it like unlocking a secret door. This alignment makes it easier for solar particles to stream into our atmosphere and light up the sky with stunning auroras.

New Moon Phases or the Moon Below Horizon

The new moon phase means the moon is practically invisible. No moonlight means the sky is as dark as it gets, and this deep darkness is perfect for making those shimmering auroras pop. Think of it like turning off the lights before a movie—everything looks better!

With the moon out of the picture, not only do auroras stand out more, but so do the stars. A new moon night offers a dazzling backdrop of stars, making the whole sky feel like a magical playground. It's like getting a double feature in the great outdoors.

Moonlight can be beautiful, but when you're trying to see the auroras, it can be a bit of a party pooper. During a new moon, there's no glare to wash out the colours of the auroras. You get to see those greens, pinks, and purples in their full, unfiltered glory.

Without the bright moonlight, your eyes can adjust to the darkness better. This improved night vision helps you catch even the faintest auroras dancing on the horizon. It's like having a superpower that lets you see the hidden wonders of the night sky.

During Geomagnetic Storms

A geomagnetic storm happens when solar wind—a stream of charged particles from the Sun—hits the Earth's magnetic field. This cosmic collision causes a big stir in the magnetosphere, lighting the sky with vibrant auroras.

During a geomagnetic storm, the aurora gets a serious power-up. The storm boosts the intensity and frequency of the auroras, making them brighter and more colourful. It's like nature cranking up the volume on its best playlist just for you!

Geomagnetic storms expand the aurora oval—the ring-shaped zone where auroras are visible. This means you might still catch the lights even if you're not close to the poles. It's like getting VIP access to a front-row seat!

Geomagnetic storms make the aurora dance in the night sky, creating stunning shapes and patterns. You might see swirls, waves, and even bursts of light. It's like watching a celestial ballet unfold right above you.

The bright, intense auroras make for amazing pictures. You'll capture those greens, pinks, and purples in all their glory. Just grab your camera and get ready for some epic shots!

Clear, Cloudless Nights

If you're itching to catch the dazzling auroras, there's one golden rule: clear, cloudless nights are your best friend.

Imagine stepping outside on a chilly night, looking up, and seeing the sky filled with vibrant colours dancing above you. That's the aurora at its best. But if the sky is full of clouds, you might miss out on this spectacular show. So, why do clear nights matter so much?

Low-Level Clouds: The Party Poopers

Low-level clouds, like stratus and cumulus, hang out close to the ground (up to 6,500 feet). These thick clouds often cover the entire sky, blocking your view entirely. It's like pulling a blanket over your head during a fireworks show—not fun!

Middle-Level Clouds: The Sneaky Spoilers

Middle-level clouds, such as altostratus and altocumulus, float between 6,500 and 20,000 feet. These clouds can be patchy but still dense enough to obscure the aurora. It's like trying to watch a movie through frosted glass—blurry and frustrating!

High-Level Clouds: The Veil of Disappointment

High-level clouds, like cirrus and cirrostratus, drift above 20,000 feet. They're thin and wispy, but don't be fooled! Even these delicate clouds can scatter the light and dull the aurora's brilliance. It's like viewing the aurora through a hazy filter—pretty, but not the whole experience.

A cloudless sky means nothing stands between you and the aurora. The lights appear brighter and more vivid, making their movements easier to follow. You get to see the aurora in all its glory, with no clouds to spoil the view.

High Kp Index Nights

The Kp index is a scale that measures geomagnetic activity, which is a fancy way of saying it tells us how intense the auroras might be. The scale runs from 0 to 9, with 0 being super quiet (no auroras) and 9 being a geomagnetic storm (aurora party!).

When the Kp index is high, the Sun gives the Earth's magnetic field a significant energy boost, making the auroras more intense, colourful, and widespread.

One of the most incredible things about high Kp index nights is that you can see auroras in places you wouldn't normally expect. When the Kp index is high, the aurora oval expands, making it possible to see the lights farther from the poles. It's like the aurora is coming to you!

3
UNDERSTANDING AURORA FORECAST PARAMETERS

Understanding the key parameters lets you know when to plan your aurora hunting adventures.

The KP Index

What it is: The Kp index measures geomagnetic activity. It ranges from 0 to 9, with higher numbers indicating stronger auroras. When solar winds hit Earth's magnetic shield, they create magnetic activity. The Kp index is a scoreboard measuring how rowdy our magnetic shield is.

Here's a breakdown:

0-2: Calm as a cat napping in the Sun. No magnetic storms here!
3-4: A gentle breeze rustling the leaves.
5-6: Auroras might start dancing in the sky.
7-9: Serious magnetic storms. Expect amazing auroras and possible satellite and power grid disruptions.

Why it matters: A higher Kp index means a better chance of seeing a dazzling aurora display. The higher the number, the wilder the space weather.

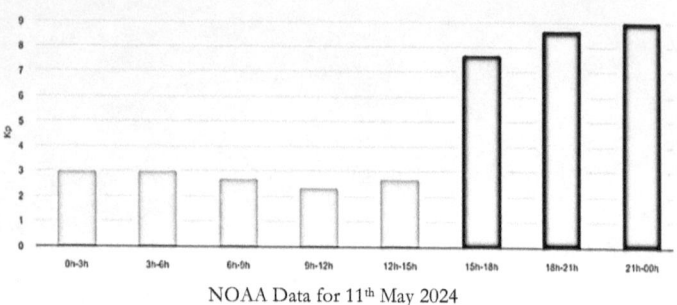

NOAA Data for 11th May 2024

Solar Wind Speed

What it is: The speed at which particles from the Sun travel towards Earth. The speed of the solar wind is crucial for predicting auroras.

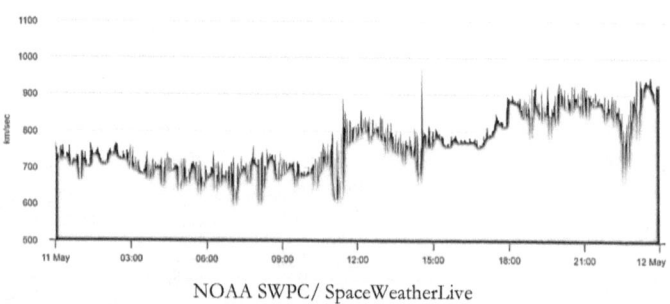

NOAA SWPC/ SpaceWeatherLive

Slow Solar Wind (200-400 km/s): Gentle breeze, faint auroras usually near the poles.

Moderate Solar Wind (400-600 km/s): Wind picks up, and there are brighter auroras in more places.

Fast Solar Wind (600+ km/s): Powerful gusts! Auroras can light up the sky far from the poles.

Why it matters: Faster solar wind speeds can lead to more intense auroras.

IMF Bt

What it is: The Interplanetary Magnetic Field (IMF) Bt measures the total strength of the magnetic field coming from the Sun.

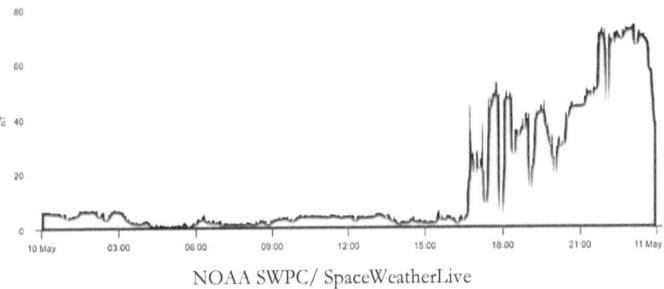

NOAA SWPC/ SpaceWeatherLive

Low IMF Bt (0-5 nT): Gentle beats, faint auroras.

Moderate IMF Bt (6-10 nT): Livlier music, more noticeable auroras.

High IMF Bt (11-20 nT): Strong beats, dynamic auroras.

Very High IMF Bt (21+ nT): Maximum volume, spectacular auroras.

Why it matters: IMF Bt values act like a volume control for the Sun's energy. Higher values mean brighter auroras.

IMF Bz

What it is: The IMF Bz component of the solar wind's magnetic field can point either north or south.

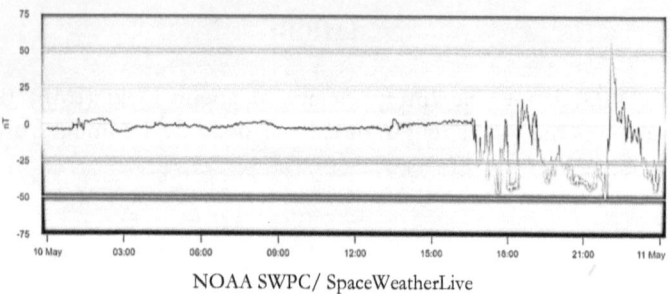

NOAA SWPC/ SpaceWeatherLive

North (Bz Positive): The solar wind bounces off Earth's magnetic shield, calm auroras.

South (Bz Negative): The solar wind connects with Earth's magnetic field, creating stunning auroras.

Why it matters: A southward Bz (negative value) interacts more effectively with Earth's magnetic field, enhancing aurora activity.

Density of Solar Wind

What it is: This measures how many solar particles are in a cubic centimetre of space.

Low Density (1-5 particles): Gentle drizzle, faint auroras.

Medium Density (6-10 particles): Steady rain, brighter auroras.

High Density (11-20 particles): Heavy downpour, spectacular auroras.

Very High Density (21+ particles): Torrential rainstorm, stunning aurora extravaganza.

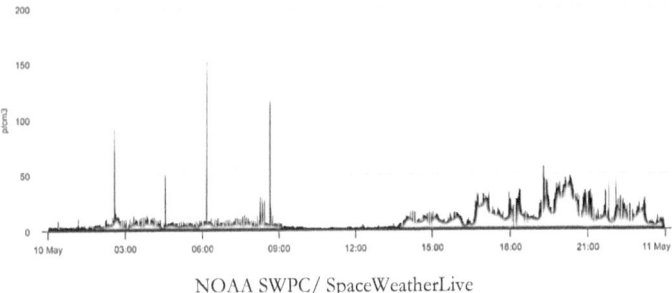

NOAA SWPC/ SpaceWeatherLive

Why it matters: Higher Density means more particles to create brighter auroras.

Auroral Oval Location

What it is: This shows where auroras will likely be visible, like a magical map for aurora hunters!

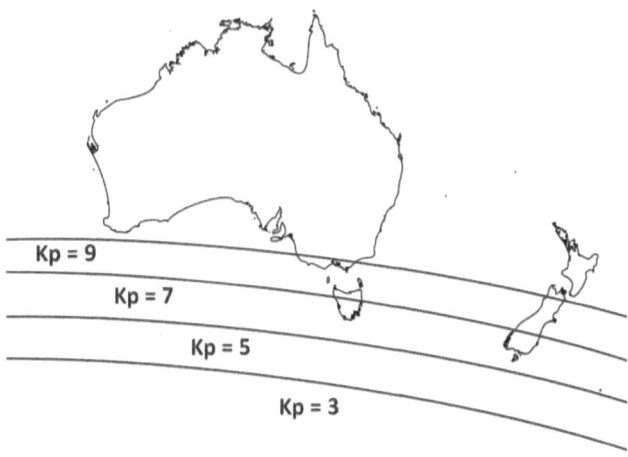

Kp = 0: 64°S, calm glow.
Kp = 1: 62.5°S, more lively.
Kp = 2: 61°S, getting brighter.
Kp = 3: 59.5°S, party starts.
Kp = 4: 58°S, getting exciting.
Kp = 5: 56.5°S, auroras are showing off.
Kp = 6: 55°S, spectacular lights.
Kp = 7: 53.5°S, sky ablaze.
Kp = 8: 52°S, peak performance.
Kp = 9: 50°S, epic display.

Why it matters: Knowing the location helps you know where to look or travel to see the lights.

Local Weather Conditions

What it is: Clear skies are essential for seeing auroras. Different types of clouds can affect visibility:

Low-Level Clouds: Thick blanket, completely blocking the view.

Medium-Level Clouds: Sheer curtain, partially blocking the view.

High-Level Clouds: Thin veil, slightly dimming the view.

Why it matters: Even the most spectacular light show can be hidden by clouds!

Hemispheric Power

What it is: Measures how much energy from the Sun hits Earth's upper atmosphere.

Low (10-20 gigawatts): Gentle and subtle auroras.
Medium (20-50 gigawatts): Brighter and more colourful

auroras.
High (50-100 gigawatts): Vibrant auroras seen further from the poles.
Very High (100+ gigawatts): Spectacular auroras light up the entire sky.

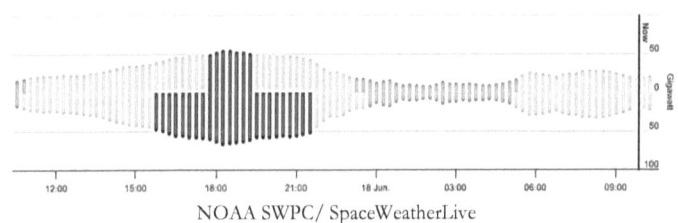

NOAA SWPC/ SpaceWeatherLive

Why it matters: Higher hemispheric power means a better chance of seeing a dazzling aurora display.

The Moon Phase

What it is: The Moon can influence Aurora's visibility.

New Moon: Dark sky is the best time to see auroras.
Crescent Moon: Dim light, still good for auroras.
Quarter Moon: Some moonlight auroras are visible but less bright.
Full Moon: Bright sky, more challenging to see auroras.

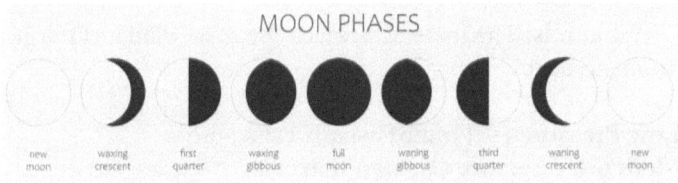

Why it matters: Less moonlight means better visibility for auroras.

Substorm Strength

What it is: Measures how powerful the aurora is at any moment.

The Bigger the Negative, the Better the Show! When the substorm strength is significantly negative, you're in for a spectacular light show.

Why it matters: Understanding substorm strength helps predict the best times to see stunning auroras.

% Negative IMF

What it is: Tells how much of the IMF is oriented southward.

0-20%: Slim chance of impressive auroras.
20-50%: Some nice auroras.
50-80%: Bright and lively auroras.
80-100%: Spectacular show!

Why it matters: Higher percentages indicate better chances for vivid auroras.

Solar Wind Pressure

What it is: The force with which the solar wind hits Earth's magnetic field.

Low Pressure (< 1 nanoPascal): Faint auroras.
Moderate Pressure (1-5 nanoPascals): Nice auroras.
High Pressure (5-10 nanoPascals): Bright and active auroras.
Very High Pressure (> 10 nanoPascals): Spectacular auroras.

Why it matters: Higher pressure boosts aurora visibility.

IMF Clock Angle θ

What it is: Interpreting the Interplanetary Magnetic Field (IMF) clock angle can be technical, but let's try to understand it in simple terms. Imagine the IMF clock angle as the hands of a cosmic clock in space. This clock helps us understand how the solar wind's magnetic field is oriented when it hits Earth. The IMF clock angle is between the Earth's magnetic field and the solar wind's magnetic field.

Perfect Alignment (Southward IMF):

Think of this as the clock hand pointing straight down (6 o'clock). When the IMF is southward, the solar wind's magnetic field aligns perfectly with Earth's. This alignment allows charged particles to stream into Earth's atmosphere, creating stunning auroras.

Not So Perfect Alignment (Northward IMF):

Now, imagine the clock hand pointing straight up (12 o'clock). When the IMF is northward, the solar wind's magnetic field opposes Earth's magnetic field, closing the door for charged particles. This means fewer or weaker auroras.

In Between (East or West IMF):

If the clock hand points to the sides (3 or 9 o'clock), the alignment could be better, but it is not completely opposed. This can still allow some particles to enter the atmosphere, leading to moderate aurora activity.

Why it matters: Check the IMF clock angle when planning your aurora hunting trip. Here's how to interpret it:

Southward (-180°): The best chance for auroras! Pack your

camera and hot cocoa.
Northward (0°): Low chance for auroras. Maybe enjoy a cozy night in.
East or West (90° or 270°): Mixed chances. Keep an eye on the sky and be ready to head out if things change.

Putting It All Together

When you check the Aurora Forecast, you'll see a mix of these parameters.

Here's a quick way to interpret them:

Kp Index of 5 or more: Get ready! Auroras might be visible.

Solar Wind Speed above 400 km/s: More excitement in the sky.

Negative Bz: Higher chances of an intense aurora.

High Solar Wind Density: Expect brighter lights.

Auroral Oval over your location: You're in the zone!

Clear Skies: Find a dark spot away from city lights.

Hemispheric Power > 50 gigawatts: Auroras might be visible.

Moon Phase:

> New moons are ideal.
> Crescent moons are good.
> Quarter moons are okay.
> Full moons are the least favourable.

Substorm Strength > -1000 nT: Auroras might be visible.

% Negative IMF 80-100% continuously for 2-3 hours: Higher chances of an aurora.

Solar Wind Pressure > 5 nanoPascals: The auroras are ramping up!

IMF clock angle θ: **Heading Southward (Towards -180°)**

Auroras are unpredictable, so some luck is involved even with all the data. But that's part of the fun! Every night under the stars could turn into an unforgettable aurora adventure. Happy Aurora Hunting!

4 AURORA APPS, WEBSITES, AND COMMUNITIES

Thanks to modern technology and vibrant online communities, chasing the Aurora Australis has never been more exciting or accessible. Let's dive into how the Aurora app, Aurora forecast websites, and Facebook community groups can turn your dream into a glowing reality.

Imagine the convenience of having a personal aurora expert right in your pocket. The Aurora apps are just that! Available for iOS and Android, they provide real-time alerts and predictions for aurora activity. Based on your preferences, the app sends instant notifications when there's a good chance of seeing the lights. You can set your location, and the app will keep you updated on the nearby aurora activity, putting you in control of your aurora-chasing experience.

Aurora Apps

1. Glendale App

CHASING AURORA AUSTRALIS

Andy Stables, the mastermind behind the Glendale Aurora App, crafted this brilliant tool with one goal: to make it easy for people worldwide to see and photograph stunning auroras. His journey began in September 2012 on the Isle of Skye, and since then, he's been dedicated to daily research to ensure the app's world-leading accuracy.

The app leverages live data from 31 magnetometers: fourteen in Norway, one in Sweden, five in Finland, five in Greenland, six in Canada, and two in Alaska. It also incorporates DSCOVR, ACE, the SDO, SOHO satellite data, real-time sun/moon positions, and twilight times.

One of the app's most engaging features is its community-driven live sighting reports. Registered users contribute real-time aurora sightings, which the app meticulously verifies using sophisticated criteria.

It's the only app in the world that provides real-time tracking of geomagnetic substorms. This feature gives users a heads-up when auroras are forming and when they're reaching their peak. With simple, colour-coded indicators, the app shows how favourable the Interplanetary Magnetic Field (IMF) looks. It also tracks negative Bz periods, detailing when these geomagnetic disturbances will hit Earth and their strength.

Android Setup

Open the Download Link via QR code above or fire up the Chrome app and head to aurora-alerts.uk. For the best experience, make sure Chrome is set as your default browser.

1. **Allow Location Access**: When prompted, allow the app to use your location 'always'. This helps the app provide accurate aurora alerts based on your location.

2. **Add to Home Screen**:
    - Scroll to the address bar at the top right.
    - Tap the icon with three vertical dots.
    - In the popup menu, select 'Add to Home Screen'.

3. **Enable Alerts**:
    - Open the app and click 'Enable Manual Alerts'. Allow the app to make updates so you stay informed.
    - Finally, click 'Enable Automatic Alerts' to ensure you get real-time notifications.

Apple / iOS Setup

Here's how to set up the Glendale Aurora App for some sky-gazing fun:

1. **Open the Download Link**: Launch Safari and go to aurora-alerts.uk.
2. **Allow Location Access**: Allow the app to use your location 'always' for precise aurora tracking.
3. **Add to Home Screen**:
    - Turn your device to landscape mode (longways) for more straightforward navigation.
    - Scroll to the address bar at the top right.
    - Tap the square icon with an arrow pointing out of it.

- In the popup menu, select 'Add to Home Screen'. Now you're all set!

Key Features:

- **Current Geomagnetic Substorm Summary**: Get the latest scoop on geomagnetic substorms, moon phase details, and when it's expected to get dark at your location.
- **Latest Alerts**: Stay informed with real-time alerts for solar flares and aurora sightings.
- **Live Aurora Reports**: Check out live reports of aurora sightings from fellow sky watchers.
- **Twilight and Moon Times**: Know exactly when twilight and moonrise will occur so you can plan your viewing.
- **Substorm Strength (24 hours)**: Monitor the strength of geomagnetic substorms over the past 24 hours.
- **IMF Bt/Bz (24 hours)**: Track the interplanetary magnetic field's behaviour for the past day.
- **IMF Clock/Theta (24 hours)**: See the IMF clock and theta angles for the last 24 hours.
- **Speed & density (24 Hour)**: Follow solar wind speed and density throughout the day.
- **TGO Stackplot (24 Hour)**: Access detailed TGO stack plots for the past 24 hours.
- **Solar Wind (2 hours, 6 hours)**: Get solar wind updates for the last 2 and 6 hours.
- **Magnetic Field (6 hours)**: View the magnetic field data for the past 6 hours.
- **Current Substorm**: Stay updated on the latest substorm activity.
- **IMF (at Earth)**: Check out the current interplanetary magnetic field at Earth.
- **Solar Wind**: Keep tabs on current solar wind conditions.

- **Coronal Holes**: Identify coronal holes and their impact.
- **Coronal Mass Ejections (CMEs) and ETA**: Track CMEs and their estimated arrival time at Earth.
- **Solar Flares and ETA**: Follow solar flares and when they'll hit Earth.
- **Long-Range Forecast**: Plan ahead with long-range space weather forecasts.

2. SpaceWeatherLive app

SpaceWeatherLive is the ultimate app for anyone eager to catch the southern lights or keep track of solar activity. With this app, users can see how active the aurora is in real time and get advanced notices for spotting the southern lights in the coming days.

Packed with space weather information for both beginners and experts, SpaceWeatherLive makes learning easy. Users can tap for a popup with more details if something is unclear, which will help them become Aurora experts quickly. Switching between auroral and solar activity modes is effortless with just one click. The app also features a unique dark mode to preserve night vision, making it perfect for aurora chasing out in the field.

Users receive free push notifications about significant space weather events like solar flares, geomagnetic storms, and earth-facing coronal holes. Notifications can be customised so users only get the alerts they care about. Alongside automated alerts, a dedicated team of space weather enthusiasts writes detailed reports during high solar or auroral activity periods.

Best of all, SpaceWeatherLive is entirely free! While there are ads, you can remove them by purchasing a subscription, which helps keep the app running smoothly.

Android Download    iOS Download

Key Features:

- **Kp-index**: Check the Kp-index to see how active the auroras are right now.
- **Real-Time Solar Wind**: Get up-to-the-minute data on solar Wind, density, and the interplanetary magnetic field (Bt, Bz).
- **Aurora Oval**: See where the aurora is likely to be visible with our aurora oval map.
- **Hemispheric Power**: Monitor the power levels in the Northern and Southern Hemispheres.
- **Disturbance Storm Time Index**: Keep track of geomagnetic storm activity with the Dst index.
- **Magnetometers - Hobart**: View real-time readings from the Hobart magnetometers.
- **Moon Phase**: Know the current moon phase to plan your night sky viewing.
- **Sunspot Regions**: Discover the latest sunspot regions on the Sun.
- **Solar Flares**: Stay updated on recent solar flares and their potential impact.
- **Solar Activity (Past Two Hours)**: Check out solar activity over the last two hours.
- **Coronal Holes**: Identify current coronal holes and their effects.
- **Coronal Mass Ejections**: Track CMEs and their expected arrival times at Earth.
- **Solar Protons**: Monitor proton flux and EPAM data to see solar proton activity.

- **Far Side**: Get information on solar activity on the Sun's far side.

3. Aurora Alerts App

Aurora Alerts is your trusty sidekick for chasing the magical southern lights! Whether you're lounging at home or on an adventure, this app keeps an eye on real-time aurora activity and gives you a heads-up if there's a chance you'll see the aurora tonight. One of its most remarkable features is a short-term forecast for the next hour, complete with weather conditions and moon illumination. So, get ready to light up your night with Aurora Alerts!

Android Download   iOS Download

Key Features:

- **Aurora Forecast %**: Check the chances of seeing the aurora both overhead and on the horizon. Get ready for some sky magic!
- **Solar Wind Data from DSCOVR**: Stay updated with real-time solar wind speed, Bz, density, and Bt. It's like having a solar weather station in your pocket.
- **Kp Index**: See the current Kp index and what it will be like in one hour. This is perfect for planning your Aurora viewing.
- **Weather and Moon Details**: Know the weather and moon phase to plan the best night for aurora watching.
- **Long Forecast**: Get long-range forecasts to see what's coming up in the sky.

- **Aurora Oval**: See where the aurora is likely to appear with our aurora oval map.
- **ACE Parameters**: Monitor key space weather parameters from the ACE satellite.
- **Weekly K Index**: Track the K index over the past week to see trends and patterns.
- **Magnetogram**: View real-time magnetograms to understand the Sun's magnetic field activity.

4. My Aurora Forecasts & Alerts

My Aurora Forecast is the ultimate app for anyone enchanted by the southern lights! Its sleek, dark design is perfect for tourists and serious aurora enthusiasts. Want to know your chances of seeing the aurora borealis or get details about solar winds and high-res sun imagery? This app has got you covered.

Key Features:

- **Current KP Index**: Check the current KP index to see your chances of catching the Southern Lights.
- **Aurora Map**: Find the best spots to view the aurora right now with our handy map.
- **Global Aurora Strength**: Explore a global map showing aurora strength based on the SWPC ovation auroral forecast.
- **Live Aurora Webcams**: Watch live aurora action from webcams around the world.
- **Viewing Probability**: See the likelihood of aurora sightings in your location.
- **Cloud Coverage**: Know the cloud coverage in your area tonight to plan the perfect Aurora viewing.
- **KP Index Forecast**: Get the KP index for the next hour and upcoming hours and days.
- **Solar Wind Data**: Stay updated with solar wind speeds, density, Bz, and Bt.

- **User-Shared Aurora Photos**: Enjoy stunning aurora photos shared by other users.
- **Sun Images**: Marvel at breathtaking images of the Sun.
- **Push Notifications**: Receive free push notifications when auroral activity spikes, so you never miss a moment of the action.

Android Download	iOS Download

Websites

While the Aurora apps are great for on-the-go updates, Aurora forecast websites are fantastic for in-depth planning. Websites like SpaceWeatherLive and NOAA provide comprehensive forecasts and valuable data for the dedicated aurora chaser. For data enthusiasts, these websites present live data and graphs showing current aurora activity. You can see real-time updates on solar winds and magnetic fields, helping you gauge the best times to catch the lights.

Glendale - Aurora-Alerts.uk

Glendale website provides all features provided on the app also on their website: aurora-alerts.uk

- **Current Geomagnetic Substorm Summary**: Get the latest scoop on geomagnetic substorms, moon phase

details, and when it's expected to get dark at your location.
- **Latest Alerts**: Stay informed with real-time alerts for solar flares and aurora sightings.
- **Live Aurora Reports**: Check out live reports of aurora sightings from fellow sky watchers.
- **Twilight and Moon Times**: Know exactly when twilight and moonrise will occur so you can plan your viewing.
- **Substorm Strength (24 hours)**: Monitor the strength of geomagnetic substorms over the past 24 hours.
- **IMF Bt/Bz (24 hours)**: Track the interplanetary magnetic field's behaviour for the past day.
- **IMF Clock/Theta (24 hours)**: See the IMF clock and theta angles for the last 24 hours.
- **Speed & density (24 Hour)**: Follow solar wind speed and density throughout the day.
- **TGO Stackplot (24 Hour)**: Access detailed TGO stack plots for the past 24 hours.
- **Solar Wind (2 hours, 6 hours)**: Get solar wind updates for the last 2 and 6 hours.
- **Magnetic Field (6 hours)**: View the magnetic field data for the past 6 hours.
- **Current Substorm**: Stay updated on the latest substorm activity.
- **IMF (at Earth)**: Check out the current interplanetary magnetic field at Earth.
- **Solar Wind**: Keep tabs on current solar wind conditions.
- **Coronal Holes**: Identify coronal holes and their impact.
- **Coronal Mass Ejections (CMEs) and ETA**: Track CMEs and their estimated arrival time at Earth.
- **Solar Flares and ETA**: Follow solar flares and when they'll hit Earth.
- **Long-Range Forecast**: Plan ahead with long-range space weather forecasts.

Space weather live

Space Weather live website provides all features provided on the app along with a few extra features:
SpaceWeatherLive.com

Key Features:

- **Kp-index**: Check the Kp-index to see how active the auroras are right now.
- **Real-Time Solar Wind**: Get up-to-the-minute data on solar wind speed, density, and the interplanetary magnetic field (Bt, Bz).
- **Aurora Oval**: Discover where the aurora is likely to be visible with our aurora oval map.
- **Hemispheric Power**: Monitor the power levels in both the Northern and Southern Hemispheres.
- **Disturbance Storm Time Index**: Keep track of geomagnetic storm activity with the Dst index.
- **Magnetometers - Hobart**: View real-time readings from the Hobart magnetometers.
- **Moon Phase**: Know the current moon phase to plan your perfect night sky viewing.
- **Sunspot Regions**: Discover the latest sunspot regions on the Sun.
- **Solar Flares**: Stay updated on recent solar flares and their potential impact.
- **Solar Activity (Past Two Hours)**: Check out solar activity over the last two hours.
- **Coronal Holes**: Identify current coronal holes and their effects.

- **Coronal Mass Ejections**: Track CMEs and their expected arrival times at Earth.
- **Solar Protons**: Monitor proton flux and EPAM data to see solar proton activity.
- **Far Side**: Get information on solar activity happening on the far side of the Sun.
- **Latest News Updates**: Stay in the loop with updates on upcoming CMEs and solar flares.
- **Radio Blackout**: Be informed about potential radio blackouts.
- **Solar Cycle Progression**: Track the progression of the solar cycle.
- **WSA-Enlil Solar Wind Prediction**: Get predictions on solar Wind from the WSA-Enlil model.
- **Webcams**: Watch live aurora action from webcams around the world.
- **Solar Activity Reports**: Access detailed reports on solar activity.
- **NOAA SWPC Alerts, Watches, and Warnings**: Receive alerts, watches, and warnings from NOAA SWPC.
- **3-Day Forecast**: Plan ahead with a 3-day space weather forecast.

Australian Space Weather Forecasting Centre: BOM

sws.bom.gov.au/Aurora

When the space weather conditions are just right, BOM lets you know where you might catch the stunning auroras—from high latitudes to equatorial regions. They even give you a heads-up 48 hours in advance if a major solar event, like a Coronal Mass Ejection (CME), is coming.

Aurora Outlooks are like your long-range forecast for these celestial events. Issued 3-7 days ahead, they predict when a big solar region might send some CME magic our way or when significant coronal holes are likely to make their mark.

Here's what you can find on the BOM Aurora page:

- **The K index**: This is the Estimated Planetary K index from NOAA/SWPC, updated every 3 hours.
- **The Kaus index**: This is the Estimated Australian Region K index from ASWFC, refreshed roughly every 5 minutes.
- **Current Solar Wind**: What's blowing in space right now!
- **Current Cloud Cover**: Clear skies or cloudy?
- **Current Moon Phase**: Is the moon adding to the light show?
- **Auroral Oval Prediction Tool**: See where auroras are most likely.
- **3-day Geomagnetic Indices**: Track geomagnetic activity.
- **Estimated Australian Region Kaus Index (3-hour data)**: Stay updated with the latest info.

NOAA Aurora Page

swpc.noaa.gov

The Space Weather Prediction Center (SWPC) is part of the National Oceanic and Atmospheric Administration. It has a dedicated Aurora Page with many forecasts that are used by websites around the world.

Key Features:
- **24-Hour Observed Space Weather Conditions**: Stay in the loop with a full day's space weather updates.
- **Latest Observed Space Weather Conditions**: Get the freshest space weather reports.
- **Predicted Space Weather Conditions**: See what's coming up in the space weather forecast.
- **Estimated K Index**: Check out the estimated K index to gauge geomagnetic activity.
- **Coronal Mass Ejections**: Big solar eruptions that can light up the skies!
- **Aurora Oval**: See where auroras are most likely to appear.
- **GOES X-Ray Flux**: Track solar X-ray activity.
- **GOES Proton Flux**: Monitor solar proton levels.
- **Estimated Planetary K Index (3 hours data)**: Get a quick update on global geomagnetic activity.
- **3-Day Forecast**: A sneak peek at the next three days of space weather.
- **Predicted Sunspot Number and Radio Flux**: Find out about upcoming sunspots and radioactivity.
- **Solar Cycle Progression**: Follow the long-term trends in solar activity.
- **27-Day Forecast**: Plan with nearly a month's space weather predictions.
- **Aurora - 30-Minute Forecast**: Get a short-term forecast for Aurora activity.
- **Geospace Geomagnetic Activity Plot**: Visualise geomagnetic activity in real-time.
- **WSA-Enlil Solar Wind Prediction**: See predictions for solar wind conditions.

Facebook Groups

One of the most exciting parts of chasing the Aurora Australis is the community of fellow aurora enthusiasts. These vibrant spaces allow you to connect, share experiences, and get tips from seasoned aurora hunters. Please always read the group rules and featured posts before posting on the group.

Group members often post real-time reports of aurora sightings, complete with photos and location details. These reports can be beneficial for finding the best viewing spots and knowing when to head out. Plus, seeing those gorgeous photos builds up the excitement! The community has valuable tips and tricks, from the best camera settings to the coziest viewing spots. Whether you're a seasoned chaser or a newbie, you'll find plenty of advice to help make your Aurora adventure successful.

There's something magical about sharing your aurora experiences with others who understand the thrill. You can swap stories, celebrate sightings, and share photos in these groups. It turns the solitary act of sky-watching into a shared adventure. Here are some of the valuable groups:

AUS & NZ

Aurora Australis

fb.com/groups/AuroraAustralia

NZ

Aurora Australis (NZ)

fb.com/groups/NZaurora

New Zealand Aurora Australis Group

fb.com/groups/NZDarkSkies

Queenstown Aurora Australis

fb.com/groups/909512465765974

TAS

Aurora Australis Tasmania

fb.com/groups/auroraaustralis

VIC

Aurora Hunters Victoria

fb.com/groups/1414520222096347

WA

Aurora Australis Western Australia

fb.com/groups/AuroraAustralisWesternAustralia

ACT/WA/ SA

Aurora Australis NSW / ACT / SA

fb.com/groups/851694958254557

5
MASTERING THE SKIES WITH CLOUD COVER FORECASTS

Cloud cover is one of the most critical factors for a successful Aurora hunt. Let's dive into how clouds can affect your adventure! When chasing Aurora Australis, you want to avoid your view blocked by pesky clouds.

Here's how different types of clouds can impact your Aurora hunting experience:

Low Clouds: The Party Crashers

Low clouds, the uninvited guests at your Aurora party, hover close to the ground, usually below 2 kilometres. Picture them as the thick, cottony blankets that cover the sky, making it a challenge to see beyond. These clouds, such as stratus clouds, are the most notorious for spoiling your Aurora viewing. If the sky is swarming with low clouds, your chances of spotting the Aurora Australis, that unpredictable beauty, are slim.

Medium Clouds: The Moody Middle

Medium clouds float higher than low clouds, typically between 2 and 6 kilometres. These include altostratus and altocumulus clouds. They can still block your view but often have gaps and can be thinner. If the night sky has medium clouds, you might still get glimpses of the Southern Lights peeking through, like a shy performer coming on stage.

High Clouds: The Spectator-Friendly Seats

High clouds are your best friends when it comes to Aurora hunting. These clouds, like cirrus and cirrostratus, hang out at altitudes above 6 kilometres. They're usually thin and wispy, like a delicate veil over the sky. High clouds often don't block your view entirely, and they can even add a bit of drama to your photos, reflecting the green and pink hues of the Aurora.

Always stay on top of cloud cover predictions. Clear skies are your golden ticket to an unobstructed view of the Aurora. But remember, the Aurora is a wild card, and the clouds can clear up unexpectedly. If you're serious about capturing the Aurora, be prepared to adapt and move to a new location with clearer skies.

Websites/ Apps to Check Cloud Cover

1. Ventusky

ventusky.com

"Ventusky" is a web app created by the Czech meteorological firm InMeteo. It provides an interactive map that allows you to explore different weather stats, such as Total Cloud Cover, Fog, Low Clouds, Middle Clouds, and High Clouds.

With the timeline at the bottom of the page, you can manage the data shown on the cloud cover map. Select the forecast period for Aurora hunting and review the cloud cover for your desired location. The time is shown based on your computer's time zone, simplifying the process of planning your adventure.

2. Cloud Free Night

cloudfreenight.com

Cloud Free Night is your go-to online weather buddy for astronomers and photographers in Australia and New Zealand! By comparing cloud forecasts from the US GFS global model and the Aussie Bureau of Meteorology's ACCESS model, you can trust the accuracy of your weather predictions.

With Cloud Free Night, you'll see detailed cloud forecast maps for specific regions in Australia and New Zealand. Plus, it provides handy five-day forecast charts for various locations, giving you a clear picture of the weather ahead. Perfect for planning your next stargazing or photo adventure!

For cloud cover, head to cloudfreenight.com/map.html

Pick your region, choose your cloud type, and jump to the timeslot you need to see the cloud cover and decide if your spot is good to go. You can easily switch between the ACCESS-G and GFS models to compare forecasts.

3. Accuweather

AccuWeather is your go-to source for all things weather! With the best global real-time and historical data, top-notch forecast models, and thorough validation results, it stands out as one of the most accurate weather companies in the world.

For your destination's current hourly cloud cover, please download the AccuWeather app or visit their website.

Android Download: iOS Download:

accuweather.com

4a. High-definition Satellite Images from BOM

Get a near real-time peek at the sky in Australia with BOM's Satellite Cloud Cover view! These stunning images come straight from the fantastic Himawari-9. Himawari-9 is a super cool geostationary weather satellite operated by the Japan Meteorological Agency (JMA). These high-tech marvels are the upgraded successors of JMA's old Multi-functional Transport Satellite (MTSAT) series, boasting significant frequency, resolution, and precision improvements.

satview.bom.gov.au

4b. MetService Cloud Cover

For the latest MetService Cloud Cover for NZ, visit: metservice.com/maps-radar/satellite/new-zealand-visible

They also have a 24-hour Cloud Cover page dedicated to Astrophotography in partnership with Samsung. Now, you can see real-time cloud cover around the clock with our dazzling NZ infrared satellite imagery, updated every 10 minutes. Just click on the markers to get the scoop on current conditions at your favourite dark sky spots so you can suit up perfectly for the weather.

Take advantage of their forecast cloud cover video to peek into the next few days.

metservice.com/maps-radar/satellite/cloud-cover

5. The Weather Channel

Refer to hourly weather with the corresponding cloud cover % on the weather channel website and app.

iOS Download: Android Download:

weather.com

Now that you're a cloud cover expert, you can use those forecasts to become a pro at planning your aurora hunting adventures!

6
LIGHTS, CAMERA, ACTION!

This chapter will explore the exciting adventure of capturing the Aurora with your camera and smartphone!

Photographing the Southern Lights is an adventure with no one-size-fits-all approach, but here are some essential tips to get you started. First off, look to the south! Find a spot with little light pollution that faces south and offers a clear view of the horizon. Make sure it's safe to be there at night—it's best to scout the location during the day to get familiar with the area. Reflective surfaces like ponds create a mirror effect that enhances and amplifies colours.

Since auroras are most active in winter, wearing warm clothes is necessary. Remember warm boots, a hat, and gloves that let you handle your camera quickly. Unlike the vibrant colours you see in photos, the aurora australis often appears as a black-and-white swirl to the naked eye. However, your camera can capture more light and reveal the colours, especially during solid events.

When driving at night in Australia, be cautious of wildlife. Kangaroos, wombats, and koalas are often active after dark, making the roads hazardous. Keep your speed in check and stay alert to avoid any unexpected encounters. Always let someone know where you're headed. It's dark, and accidents can happen. Bring a friend or two, not just for company but for safety, too!

Capturing the Aurora with Your Camera

DSLR or Mirrorless Camera—You don't need the latest and greatest model; ensure it can handle long exposure shots. Pick a landscape scene that would be interesting even without the Aurora when setting up your shot. You'll be amazed at how incredible it looks with the Aurora in the frame.

Know Your Settings

Before your trip, take the time to learn which camera settings will help you capture the best photos. Please get familiar with your camera's settings and practice using it in the dark. That way, you won't be fumbling around while the Lights are dancing in front of you.

Batteries and Memory Cards

Cold weather drains batteries fast, so make sure your camera is fully charged and bring extra batteries. Use a high-capacity memory card or bring a few spares to store all your RAW shots of the Aurora.

Tripod

You'll need a sturdy tripod to keep your camera still, a camera that's great in low light, and a lens with a wide aperture to let in lots of light. Your tripod doesn't have to be the priciest, but sturdier ones hold up better in windy conditions. If it's not rigid enough, hang something heavy from the hook under the central column—your backpack, a water bottle, or a rock.

Lenses

For lenses, go for a fast, wide-angle one. An f/2.8 or lower is perfect. You generally don't want to shoot the Aurora with a focal length longer than 35mm. 14mm lenses are also popular. A fisheye lens can also be handy for those nights when the aurora activity is off the charts.

A wide-angle lens lets you capture more of the Aurora and the stunning landscape in your shots. Having one in your camera kit is perfect for making the most of the natural composition that Australia and New Zealand's landscapes offer. It allows you to frame the breathtaking celestial spectacle and the beautiful scenery as much as possible.

Remote

An intervalometer allows the camera to take continuous shots, which is ideal for creating time-lapse videos. Plus, it lets the photographer step away and enjoy the show! A remote shutter release cable or wireless remote helps reduce camera vibrations from pressing the shutter button. Many photographers prefer continuous shooting mode, allowing them to relax and watch the Aurora while the camera does all the work. The self-timer Mode (2 seconds) also ensures the camera waits 2 seconds before capturing the exposure after the shutter button is pressed.

Infinity Focus

Focusing in the dark can be tricky since auto-focus won't work.

Here's how to nail it:

Focus on a Star: Focus on a star and make it as sharp as possible. If that's impractical, wind your focus to infinity (look for the sideways figure 8 symbol).

Manual Focus Without Infinity: If your lens doesn't have the infinity option, set the camera to manual focus, open the aperture as wide as possible, and turn on the live view. Point your camera at the sky and find a bright star in the field of view. Center the star and zoom in on the live view (using the camera controls, not the lens zoom ring).

Fine-Tune Focus: Gently adjust the focusing ring until the star is sharp. Once you've got it, carefully tape down the focus and the zoom ring (if there is one) on your lens.

Manual Mode:

Manual Mode on your camera gives you complete control over all the settings—aperture, shutter speed, white balance, exposure, and ISO. You can adjust these settings to get the exact exposure and effect you want for your photos. It's great for creative control, allowing you to adapt to lighting conditions and capture the perfect shot.

White Balance

White balance is crucial for capturing the true colours of the Aurora. It adjusts the colour temperature of your photos to ensure the colours look natural. Different settings work for different lighting conditions:
- Under a full moon, use a warmer temperature (5700-5900K); without moonlight, go cooler (4200-4500K).

Ultimately, choose the setting that best matches your taste.
Set the white balance to match your tastes and what looks best to you.

ISO

ISO is a camera setting that controls the sensor's sensitivity to light. A lower ISO number (like 100) means less sensitivity, which is great for bright conditions. A higher ISO number (like 3200) increases sensitivity, making it easier to take photos in low light, but it can also add graininess.

When setting your ISO, you must decide based on how much noise your camera can handle. The higher the ISO, the more light your camera can capture. Generally, ISO 1600-3200 is a good range. If the Aurora is faint or invisible to the naked eye, crank the ISO up to 6400 or higher. You can lower the ISO to 400-800 if the Aurora is bright and easily visible. Adjust to get the best shot!

Aperture (f-stop)

Aperture is how wide the lens opens when taking a photo. A wider aperture (lower f-stop number) lets in more light, which is excellent for low-light conditions.

For aurora photography, you want the lens to be as wide open as possible to capture more light. Typically, we recommend an aperture of about f/1.8 - f/2.8. Some lenses can open more comprehensively, but many zoom lenses can't reach f/2.8. That's okay—experiment and see what works best for you! Set your aperture (f-stop) to at least f/4 to let in enough light to capture the Aurora, but aim for f/2.8 or lower f-stop. There are prime lenses that stop down to f1.4.

Shutter Speed

Shutter speed determines how long the camera's sensor is exposed to light. A faster shutter speed captures quick moments, while a slower shutter speed lets in more light and captures movement over time.

For bright and active auroras, try a shutter speed of 3-10 seconds; for slow-moving auroras, go for 12-20 seconds; and for faint auroras, extend it to 20-25 seconds. Since the Aurora constantly moves, the faster the shutter speed, the more detail you'll capture. Feel free to adjust the shutter speed based on your results.

Shooting RAW

Shooting in RAW Mode is crucial because it captures all the data from your camera's sensor without any compression. This means you get the highest-quality image with the most detail and the best possible dynamic range. RAW files also allow for greater flexibility in post-processing, letting you adjust exposure, white balance, and other settings without losing image quality. RAW files give you more control over your final photo, making them essential for serious photographers.

500 Rule

The 500 Rule helps you avoid star trails in night sky photos. Divide 500 by your lens's focal length for the longest exposure time in seconds. For example, if you're using a 20mm lens, $500 \div 20 = 25$ seconds. So, you can be exposed for up to 25 seconds without getting star trails.

For cropped sensor cameras, you need to account for the crop factor. Divide 500 by the effective focal length (lens focal length multiplied by the crop factor). For instance, with a 20mm lens on a camera with a 1.5x crop factor would be $500 \div (20 \times 1.5) = 16.7$ seconds. So, you can expose for about 17 seconds without getting star trails.

Capturing the Aurora with Your Smartphone

You don't need a fancy camera to capture stunning shots of the Aurora! Your smartphone can do the trick. With its night mode and long exposure settings, you can snap vibrant photos of the Southern Lights.

iPhone

Night photography can be tricky, but your iPhone makes it a breeze to snap stunning shots of the Southern Lights, even for beginners. Here's how to make the most of your iPhone's capabilities:

1. Enable Night Mode: Night Mode will automatically turn on in low-light conditions. Look for the Night Mode icon (a moon) in the top left corner. This Mode keeps the camera sensor open longer to let in more light, capturing more detail through long exposure. You'll need to maximise this exposure time for the best results with the Southern Lights. This feature is available on every iPhone since the iPhone 11, and the latest models have even better photo quality.

2. Mount Your iPhone on a Tripod: While you can shoot handheld, a sturdy tripod will give you the best, most precise results. Even a slight movement can blur your photo. If you don't have a tripod, try placing your iPhone on a stable surface. You can also use your Apple Watch to trigger the camera remotely to prevent accidental shakes.

3. Use the 1x Lens: The 1x wide-angle lens is the best for low-light photography. While you can use other lenses, the 1x lens will give you the brightest and clearest shots.

4. Manually Focus: Tap on the screen to focus on your subject. Whether it's an interesting object in the foreground or a selfie under the Southern Lights, make sure your focus is spot on. If you capture the sky, your iPhone will automatically focus to infinity.

5. Adjust Shutter Speed: After a test shot, check the Southern Lights' visibility. If they're faint, increase the shutter speed by swiping up in the Camera app and tapping the Night Mode icon. A tripod can take longer exposures, capturing more light and detail.

6. Shoot in RAW: For the best control over your photos, shoot in RAW. Turn this on in Settings > Camera > Formats > Apple ProRAW. This allows greater flexibility in post-processing with apps like Adobe Lightroom Mobile.

Android

Get ready to snap some stunning Southern Lights photos with your Android! Here's how to do it:

1. Tripod and Phone Holder: Invest in a light, compact tripod that fits in your luggage. Make sure you have a phone holder that tightens with a screw. If you have a spring-loaded holder, use an elastic band to make it more secure. You don't want your phone to fall off in the middle of a great shot!

2. Focus for Clarity: Tap on your screen to focus on a point, like a star or something in the distance. This ensures your image is sharp and clear. You don't want to set up everything perfectly and end up with a blurry photo!

3. Use Your Primary Lens: Use your primary lens for the best quality photos. Avoid using a super-wide lens, as it's not as good in low-light conditions.

4. Shoot in RAW: Enable RAW shooting mode to give yourself more flexibility when editing your photos later.

5. Enable Night Mode: Turn your Android camera app on night mode. Set your ISO to 1600 or higher for better low-light performance. Adjust the white balance to around 3200K to make your image look natural.

6. Adjust Shutter Speed: Set your camera to 'Professional' or 'Manual' Mode. Toggle the 'MF' icon to focus the camera and turn off the flash. Set the shutter speed for bright and colourful lights to 1-5 seconds. For dimmer lights, lengthen it to 20-30 seconds.

7. Rotate Your Device: Turn your device horizontally to capture a wider scene.

Samsung Galaxy Expert RAW

Expert RAW is an excellent camera app for Samsung Galaxy that lets you take high-quality HDR photos that you can edit later in detail. You can download it from the Galaxy Store and use it on Galaxy S20 or later models.

You get JPEG and RAW (Linear DNG 16-bit) files when you shoot with Expert RAW. Unlike JPEGs, RAW files keep all the uncompressed image data, so you have more editing flexibility.

You can also directly control settings like ISO, shutter speed, white balance, exposure, and focus for more professional shots. Plus, with the 'Special photo options' feature, you can capture astrophotography and multiple exposures.

How to Use Expert RAW:

Open the Expert RAW app.
Tap the settings icon.
Turn on "Special photo options".
Choose Astrophotography mode and adjust the focus, white balance, and exposure time to capture the night sky.

Recommended Settings:

Shutter Speed: Start with 10 seconds and adjust based on the Aurora's intensity.
ISO: Begin at 800, change as needed.

White Balance: Set to 3900K.
Focus: Center.
Everything else: Leave on auto.
File Type: RAW image.

Editing Aurora Photos

If you want to edit Aurora photos on your smartphone, check out the built-in editing tools in the iPhone and Android camera apps. Use Lightroom's advanced features for camera photos or event smartphone photos to make your pictures genuinely excellent.

Here are some fun Lightroom features you'll want to play around with:

Adjust White Balance: This one's a bit tricky because it sets the entire style of your image. There's no "one size fits all" setting. Your values will change depending on whether you're under a full moon or no moon at all. Remember, your final white balance is all about your taste!

Adjust Exposure: This tool brightens or darkens your entire photo. It helps bring out details in both shadows and highlights. Use it to fix lighting issues and make your photo pop.

Dehaze: Clear up foggy or misty scenes and add contrast and clarity with this tool. Perfect for enhancing landscapes and making your photos vibrant.

Highlights and Shadows: Balance the brightest and darkest parts of your photo. Highlights bring back details in overexposed spots, while shadows reveal details in the darker areas. These sliders help you achieve a balanced and detailed image.

Contrast: Adjust the difference between light and dark areas. Increasing contrast adds depth and drama while reducing it creates a softer look. Use this tool to enhance the overall impact of your photos.

Blacks and Whites: Use these sliders to control the darkest and brightest parts of your photo. Fine-tuning them helps balance contrast and detail in shadows and highlights, adding depth and richness to your image.

Vibrance and Saturation: Adjust the intensity of colours. Saturation affects all colours equally, while vibrance boosts more muted colours and protects skin tones. These tools make your photos vivid and lively without overdoing it.

Clarity and Texture Enhance details in your photo. Clarity adds mid-tone contrast for a sharper look, which is great for landscapes. Texture brings out fine details without affecting overall contrast. Use these to add crispness and depth.

Adjust Individual Colours: Use the HSL panel to tweak specific colours. Change the hue, adjust saturation, and modify luminance to make colours lighter or darker. This tool gives you precise control over your colour palette for a customised look.

CHASING AURORA AUSTRALIS

7
THE EPIC GEOMAGNETIC STORM OF MAY 2024

In May 2024, a rare and powerful geomagnetic storm, the strongest in over two decades, left millions worldwide in awe. This intense G5 storm, a once-in-a-lifetime spectacle, produced a spectacular Aurora Australis and Aurora Borealis display on May 11-12, visible even in regions where auroras are rare. The remarkable event was caused by a massive sunspot cluster (AR3664) 15-16 times Earth's size, unleashing solar eruptions towards Earth, resulting in the most significant geomagnetic storm in almost twenty years. This storm was the most intense since the Halloween solar storms of 2003.

The Sun is currently approaching the peak of its Solar Maximum Cycle. On May 8, 2024, a highly active solar region, AR3664, released multiple Coronal Mass Ejections (CMEs). These were triggered by a powerful X-Class flare (X5.8) and several M-class solar flares directed towards Earth. As they travelled, these CMEs combined into a large mass of plasma that reached Earth on May 11. The plasma that entered Earth's magnetic field was dense and packed with charged particles, crucial for generating vibrant auroras.

The interplanetary magnetic field reached 73 nT (nanotesla). The orientation of the Earth's magnetic field (Bz) was strongly southward at -50 nT, which caused it to be overwhelmed by charged particles. This, combined with high solar wind density and 750–800 km/s speeds, classified the event as a G5-class geomagnetic storm (Kp = 9). As a result, the Aurora Oval expanded, making auroras visible in numerous locations worldwide. In Australia, auroras were seen as far north as Townsville and Mackay in Queensland. New Zealand, Chile, Argentina, South Africa, Uruguay, and Namibia also had the privilege of witnessing the beautiful auroras in the Southern Hemisphere.

On May 14, 2024, the most active solar region rotated away from Earth, and an X8.7 flare erupted. If it had been Earth-directed, we might have had another record-breaking storm, a prospect that keeps us on the edge of our seats. But for now, we can marvel at the unforgettable light show of May 2024, and eagerly await the next celestial spectacle.

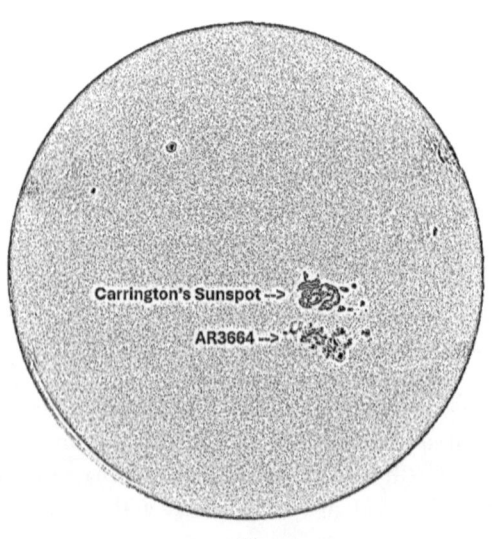

1859 Carrington Event

The 1859 Carrington Event was a supercharged solar storm that created one of the most spectacular aurora displays ever recorded. Here's why it's still talked about today, especially when it comes to auroras.

First, let's set the scene. In late August 1859, astronomers observed giant sunspots on the Sun. Then, on September 1, a massive solar flare erupted. This flare was so intense that it was visible to the naked eye in broad daylight! It sent a gigantic wave of solar particles hurtling towards Earth, which hit just 17.6 hours later.

When these particles collided with Earth's magnetic field, the result was an awe-inspiring light show. The auroras from the Carrington Event were seen as far south as the Caribbean. People like Cuba, Jamaica, and even Hawaii were treated to skies filled with dazzling colours. In the northern hemisphere, the auroras were so bright that people in the northeastern United States could read newspapers at night by their light!

But the Carrington Event wasn't just about pretty lights. It also caused significant disruptions. Telegraph systems around the world went haywire. Some telegraph operators reported sparks flying from their equipment, and some were even able to send messages despite their batteries being disconnected.

CHASING AURORA AUSTRALIS

8
WHAT MAKES AURORA HUNTING VERY ADDICTIVE?

Aurora hunting is a unique adventure akin to chasing the sky's most mesmerizing light show. Once you've tasted this exclusive experience, it's hard to resist its allure. Let's delve into the irresistible charm of aurora hunting!

The Thrill of the Chase

Imagine yourself as a detective on the hunt for the most elusive, magical phenomenon in the night sky. The thrill of predicting where and when the auroras will appear is like solving a cosmic puzzle. Each successful sighting is a triumphant moment that leaves you yearning for more.

The Unpredictable Show

No two auroras are exactly alike. They come in various shapes, colours, and patterns, making each experience unique. One night, you might see delicate green curtains rippling across the sky. The next, you could witness vivid pink and purple streaks dancing like celestial ballet. This unpredictability keeps you on your toes and always wanting to see what the sky will offer next.

Nature's Light Show

Auroras are nature's most breathtaking displays, often likened to a "living" light show. Observing them dance and shimmer across the sky is akin to witnessing a masterpiece painted in real-time. This captivating beauty is a visual delight that can leave you spellbound and eager for another glimpse.

The Perfect Excuse for Adventure

Aurora hunting often takes you to remote, beautiful locations with clear, dark skies. These adventures can lead you to many beautiful landscapes. The journey becomes part of the thrill, combining the love of nature, travel, and the excitement of the hunt.

Bonding with Fellow Hunters

Aurora hunting is not just a hobby; it's a social experience. Joining fellow enthusiasts, sharing tips, and celebrating sightings together creates a strong sense of community and camaraderie. These shared moments and friendships enhance your connection to the hunt and make it even more enjoyable.

Capturing the Magic

Photographing the aurora is a hobby within a hobby. Capturing the perfect shot of these glowing lights is both challenging and rewarding. Every successful photo becomes a cherished memory, and the desire to improve your skills and capture even more breathtaking images keeps you hooked.

The Emotional High

There's an emotional aspect to aurora hunting that's hard to describe. The awe and wonder you feel when you finally see the sky light up with vibrant colours can be deeply moving. It's a moment of pure joy and amazement that you want to experience over and over again.

A Cosmic Connection

Aurora hunting connects you to the larger universe. Understanding the science behind the auroras and witnessing them firsthand can make you feel more connected to the cosmos. It's a reminder of the incredible beauty and complexity of the universe, sparking a sense of curiosity and wonder that never fades.

Once you start, it's hard to resist the allure of the dancing lights in the sky. Happy Aurora Hunting!

CHASING AURORA AUSTRALIS

9
AURORA HUNTING NEEDS A LOT OF PATIENCE

Aurora hunting is like fishing for the sky's most magical light show—you need a lot of patience, but the reward is always worth it. Let's explore why patience is a virtue in this cosmic quest and how it makes the experience even more exciting!

The Waiting Game

Picture yourself bundled up in warm clothes, standing under a vast, starry sky. You've got your hot cocoa, your camera ready, and a hopeful heart. But here's the catch: auroras don't run on a schedule. You might have to wait hours, even all night, for them to appear. This waiting game can test your patience but is also part of the thrill.

The Anticipation Builds

Every little change in the sky gets your heart racing as you wait. Did you see a faint glow on the horizon? Was that a shooting star or the first sign of the aurora? The anticipation builds, making the eventual sighting even more rewarding. It's like waiting for a surprise gift—you know it's coming, and the suspense is half the fun.

The Art of Relaxation

While waiting, you can slow down and soak in the beauty around you. The night sky is a wonder, filled with countless stars, constellations, and sometimes even the Milky Way. This quiet time can be relaxing and meditative, giving you a break from the hustle and bustle of everyday life.

A Test of Perseverance

Aurora hunting can sometimes be a test of perseverance. You may have gone out several nights in a row but have yet to succeed. But true aurora hunters know that persistence pays off. You're one step closer to witnessing the magic each night you head out. And when it finally happens, it feels like a triumph—a reward for your dedication and patience.

The Community of Hunters

One of the best parts of aurora hunting is sharing the experience with fellow enthusiasts. You're not in this alone! Whether you're with friends and family or meeting new people at popular viewing spots, there's a sense of camaraderie. Sharing stories, tips, and even the waiting process can make the time pass quickly and turn the experience into a social adventure.

The Big Reveal

When the auroras finally appear, all that waiting and patience pay off. The sky lights up with vibrant colours, dancing and shimmering in a way that takes your breath away. It's a moment of pure awe and joy, and knowing you waited for it makes it even sweeter.

A Lesson in Nature's Pace

Aurora hunting teaches you to appreciate nature's rhythms. Not everything happens instantly, and that's okay. The best things often come to those who wait; the aurora is a perfect example. Patience helps you connect with the natural world and appreciate its wonders more profoundly and meaningfully.

So, if you're ready to embark on the adventure of aurora hunting, pack your patient warm clothes and a camera. Embrace the waiting game, enjoy the journey, and prepare for one of the night sky's most magical experiences. Happy Aurora Hunting!

10
STEVE

Meet STEVE, the enigmatic celestial phenomenon that defies the norms of the aurora. STEVE, an acronym for Strong Thermal Emission Velocity Enhancement, is not your run-of-the-mill aurora. It's a one-of-a-kind spectacle that paints the night sky with a touch of mystery. But what exactly is STEVE, and what sets it apart? Let's embark on a journey to uncover its intriguing nature!

What is STEVE?

Picture a slender band of light stretching across the night sky. Unlike the usual green and red curtains of the aurora, STEVE bathes the sky in a mesmerizing purplish hue with a hint of green. It's as if someone has painted a vibrant streak across the heavens. STEVE can even sport a unique 'picket fence' pattern of green vertical stripes, adding to its allure.

The Mystery of STEVE

Initially mistaken by amateur sky watchers for a new type of aurora, STEVE was swiftly recognized by scientists as a groundbreaking atmospheric phenomenon. Unlike traditional auroras, which are a result of charged particles from the sun interacting with Earth's atmosphere, STEVE is a product of a distinct process. This unique discovery has opened up new avenues for scientific exploration, making STEVE a significant and captivating subject of study.

What Causes STEVE?

STEVE's light show happens because of fast-moving particles in the upper atmosphere.

High-Speed Particles: STEVE occurs when a high-speed flow of hot particles in the upper atmosphere travels at thousands of miles per hour. These particles create friction with the cooler air around them, causing the air to glow.

Ion Drift: The purplish ribbon of STEVE is caused by a phenomenon known as ion drift. This is when ions (charged particles) rush through the Earth's magnetic field, heating the atmosphere and making it emit light.

Different Altitudes: The green picket fence pattern sometimes seen with STEVE is created at a different altitude than the purple ribbon. This green light is caused by energetic particles colliding with oxygen in the atmosphere, much like the regular aurora.

Why STEVE is Special

STEVE is not just a pretty sight; it's a scientific puzzle. It defines the characteristics of a typical aurora, making it a rare and unique event that sparks scientific curiosity. Researchers are still unravelling its secrets, but one thing's sure: when STEVE graces the sky, it's a breathtaking spectacle that leaves us in awe!

So, the next time you find yourself under the stars, keep an eager eye out for a vivid, purplish streak with a hint of green. You might just be fortunate enough to witness the magical emergence of STEVE, the sky's exclusive light show. Remember, STEVE's appearances are a delightful surprise, adding a thrilling element to your stargazing escapades!

11
PRIME AURORA LOCATIONS - NZ

QR Code for 180+ NZ Aurora locations

Here are some prime spots to catch the show in New Zealand, provided the skies are clear and the whims of geomagnetic storms are in your favour.

Pro tip: Safety is paramount! Before your Aurora Australis adventure, make sure to thoroughly inspect your chosen site during the day to spot any potential hazards. Remember to follow access signs and always prioritize your safety!

While we've done our best with the map, it's important to note that the accuracy of the information can't be guaranteed. We encourage you to always double-check for the most up-to-date details.

Aurora Locations in Stewart Island / Rakiura

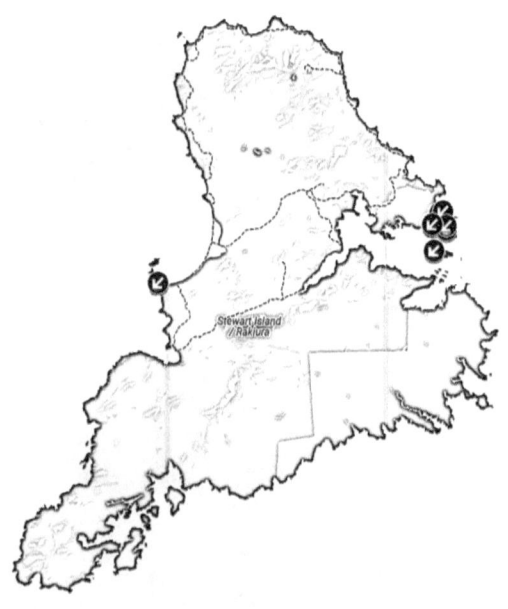

Observation Rock Viewpoint

Ringaringa Beach

Wohler's Monument

Butterfield Beach

Bragg Bay

Golden Bay Wharf

Watercress Beach

The Gutter

Boulder Beach

CHASING AURORA AUSTRALIS

Aurora Locations in Orepuki, Pahia, Rowallan, and Te Waewae

South Coastal Track

Bluecliffs Beach

Elephant Rock

McCracken's Rest

Gemstone Beach

Cosy Nook (cove)

Aurora Locations in Invercargill, Tihaka, Riverton / Aparima, Taramoa, Murihiku, Greenpoint, and Bluff

Tihaka Beach Road

Balancing Rock

Howell Point Lookout

Oreti River Bridge

Oreti Beach

Greenpoint Ship Graveyard

Bluff Hill Lookout

Stirling Point

Aurora Locations in Fortrose, Otara, Slope Point, and Curio Bay

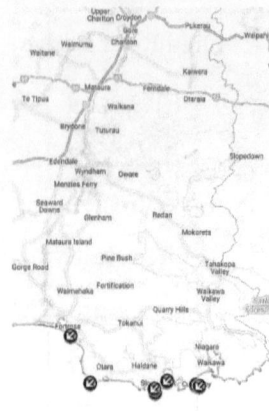

Slope Point Parking

The Southern Most Point of the South Island of New Zealand

Cliffs at Fortrose (Mataura River Mouth)

Freedom Camping Site

Waipapa Point Lighthouse

Petrified Forest Curio Bay

The Headland

CHASING AURORA AUSTRALIS

Aurora Locations in Chaslands, Papatowai, Otago, Purakaunui, Hinahina, New Haven, and Ahuriri Flat

Florence Hill Lookout

Tautuku Viewing Platform

Tautuku Beach

Skeleton Point Lookout

Nugget Point Lighthouse

Surat Bay Beach

CHASING AURORA AUSTRALIS

Jack's Blowhole

Nugget Point

Nugget Point Car Park

Helena Falls Beach

Tautuku Beach Parking

Tahakopa Beach

Aurora Locations in Toko Mouth, Otago, Glenledi, and Akatore

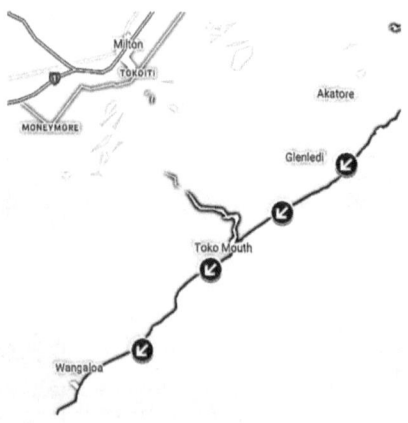

CHASING AURORA AUSTRALIS

Bull Creek Scenic Reserve

Chrystalls Beach

Mitchell Rocks

Measly Beach

Aurora Locations in Otago, Dunedin, Sandfly Bay, Sandymount, and Cape Saunders

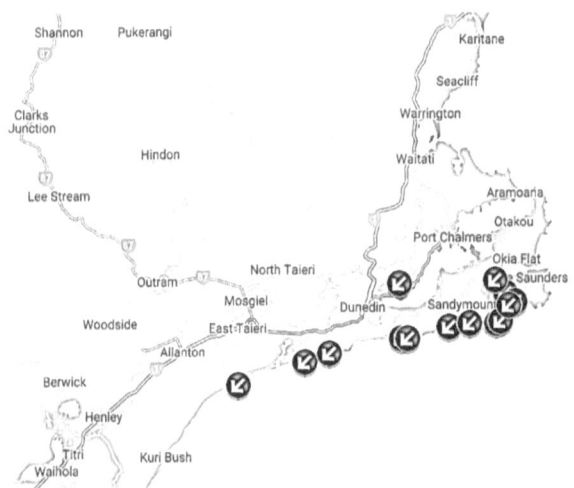

Rock View Point

Smaills Beach

CHASING AURORA AUSTRALIS

Hoopers Inlet

Tunnel Beach Walking Track

Signal Hill Lookout

Tomahawk Beach

Sandymount - Allan's Beach Lookout

Sandfly Bay

Lovers Leap

Boulder Beach

Blackhead Surfing Beach

Hooper's Inlet Shed

Allans Beach

Aurora Locations in Te Anau

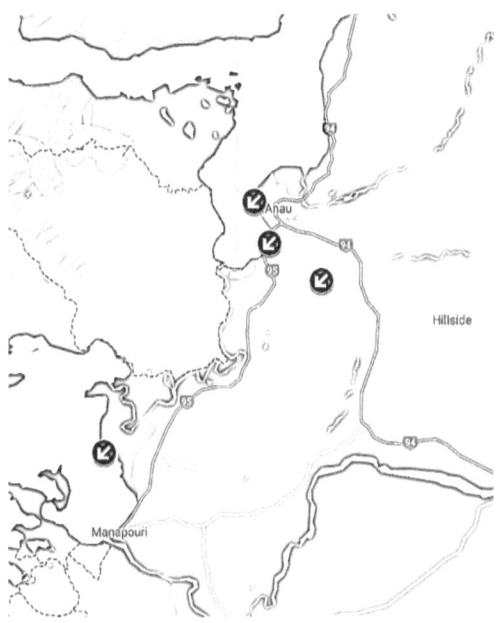

Lake Henry Viewing Deck

Free Barbecue
(Location Name)

Te Anau Lions Lookout Point

Supply Bay Recreational Area Parking

Aurora Locations in Mount Creighton, Kingston, Roaring Meg, Mount Pisa, Wānaka, Lake Hāwea, and Albert Town

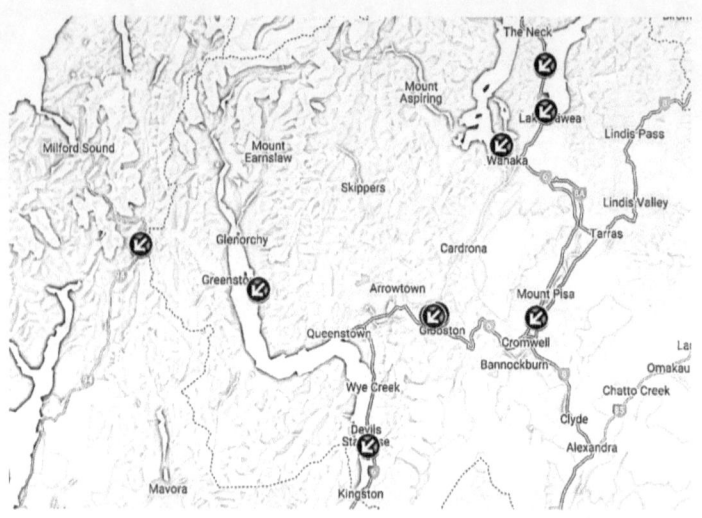

Beacon Point

Crown Range Summit

Devil's Staircase Lookout Point

Lake Hawea Lookout

Lake Gunn North
Viewpoint

Crown Range Road
Scenic Lookout

Lookout point
(Mount Creighton)

Wright Lookout

45th Parallel
South Marker

Peacemaker

Aurora Locations in Lake Tekapo, Ben Ohau, Pukaki, Glentanner, and Tekapo

The Church of
the Good Shepherd

Lupins Flower-sea

Tekapo Canal

Pukaki swing

Lake Pukaki Lookout

Lake Tekapo
Peninsula Walkway

Tapataia Mahaka Peter's
Lookout
(Lake Pukaki Viewpoint)

Cowans Hill

Glentanner Lookout

Mt Cook High Peak

Aurora Locations in Christchurch, Lowcliffe, Wakanui, Southbridge, Leeston, Birdlings Flat, Te Oka, Akaroa, and Kennedys Bush

Birdlings Flat Beach

Lowcliffe beach

Tambledown Bay

Omahu Bush Reserve / Gibraltar Rock Car Park

Kaitorete Spit

Akaroa Head Scenic Reserve

Lakeside Domain
Freedom Camping

Coopers Lagoon

Wakanui Beach

Aurora Locations in Domett, Peketā, Kaikōura, Half Moon Bay, and Marlborough

Dr James A Mills

Ward Beach

A Harveys Head

Kaikoura Lookout

Whalers Bay

Luca's Beach

Pinnacle Rock

Ohau Point Lookout

Point Gibson Lighthouse

Seal beach

Aurora Locations in Dillmanstown

Kapitea Reservoir   Dillmans Dam

Aurora Locations in Wellington, Lower Hutt, and Wainuiomata Coast

CHASING AURORA AUSTRALIS

Hinds Point

Baring Head Lighthouse

Pariwhero/Red Rocks

Taputeranga Snorkel Trail

Princess Beach

Wainuiomata Beach

Tongue Point

Owhiro Bay Beach

Lake Ferry Beach

Te Raekaihoe

Whangaimoana Beach

Ataturk Memorial Park

CHASING AURORA AUSTRALIS

Orchy Cres Lookout

Lion's rock

Point view Breaker Bay

Owhiro Bay Parade

Te Kopahou Visitor Centre

Beach access carpark (Wainuiomata Coast)

Red Rocks - Seals

Aurora Locations in Cape Palliser, White Rock, Tora, and Te Awaiti

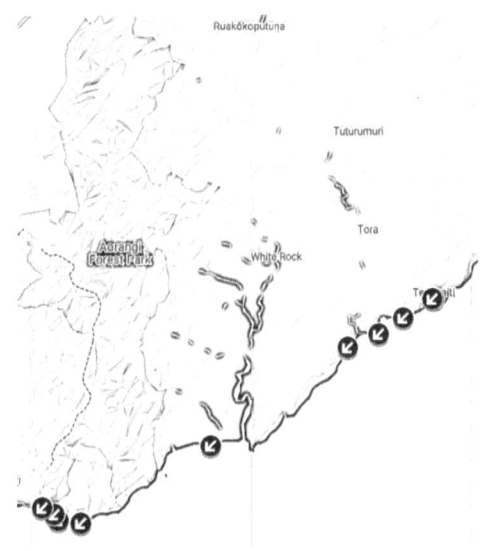

Te Awaiti Beach

Sandy Bay Recreational Reserve

Manurewa Point Recreation Reserve

Tora Recreation Reserve

CHASING AURORA AUSTRALIS

Sea lions view point

Cape Palliser Lighthouse Car Park

Mangatoetoe Beach

White Rock

Mangatoetoe Entrance Carpark

Aurora Locations in Castlepoint

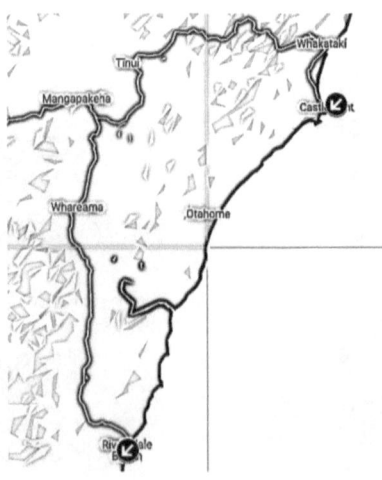

Riversdale Beach

Castlepoint Lighthouse

Aurora Locations in Herbertville and Hawke's Bay

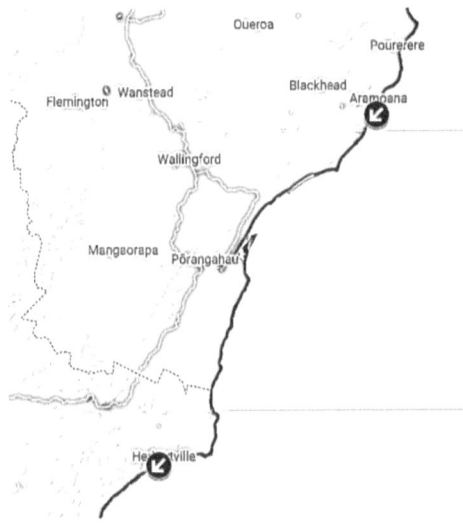

Herbertville Monument

Blackhead Beach

Aurora Locations in Whanganui, Pākaraka, Waiinu Beach and Patea

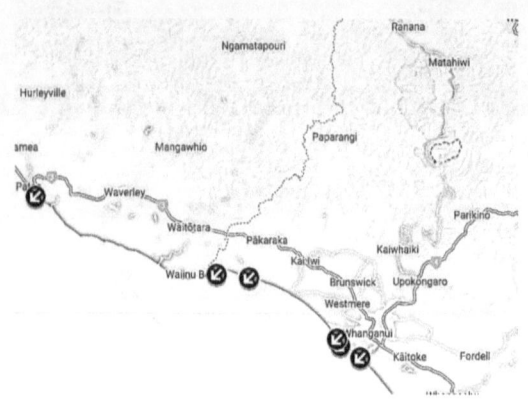

Castlecliff Beach

North Mole

Riverview Lookout

Tuuaropaki

Ototoka Beach

South Beach

Aurora Locations in Hāwera, Taranaki, and Ōpunake

Pouakai Circuit - Henry Peak Lookout

Ohawe Beach

Sandy Bay Beach Reserve

Waihi Beach

Mount Egmont viewing platform

Aurora Locations in Gisborne, Nūhaka, and Tolaga Bay

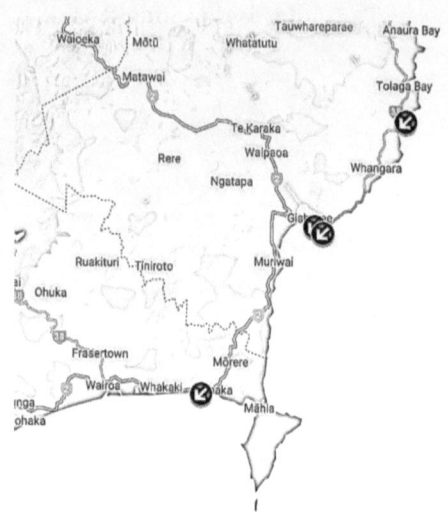

Sponge Bay Beach

Titirangi

Rocket Launch Viewing Area

Waihau Bay Beach

Aurora Locations in Auckland, Āwhitu, and Muriwai

O'neill Bay Lookout

Whatipu Beach

Donald Mclean Lookout

Ninepin Rock

Hamilton's Gap

Karioitahi Beach

Aurora Locations in Northland

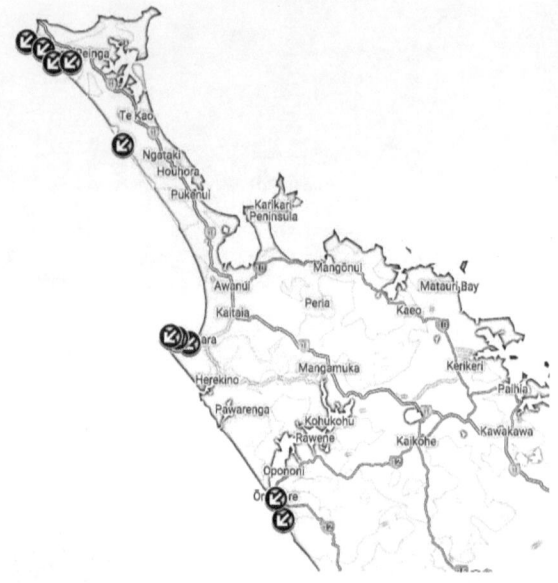

Kahokawa Beach

Cape Maria Van Diemen

Ahipara sand dunes

Ninety Mile Beach

Paengarēhia / Twilight Beach

Three trees Ahipara view

Waimamaku Beach

Giant Sand Dunes

Pakia Hill Lookout

CHASING AURORA AUSTRALIS

12
PRIME AURORA LOCATIONS - TAS

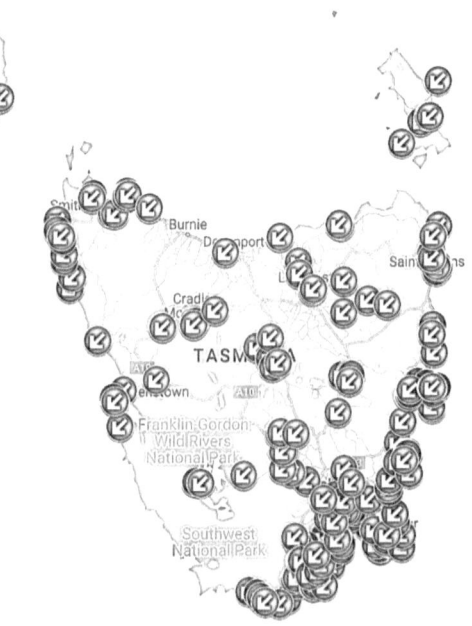

QR Code for 210+ TAS Aurora locations

Aurora Locations in South East Cape

Turua Beach

Granite Beach

Prion Beach

Lion Rock

Osmiridium Beach

Motts Beach

Aurora Locations in Southport

Southport Bluff Beach

Elliott Beach

Southport Boat Ramp and Jetty

Telstra Payphone

Southport Jetty

Roaring Beach Lookout

Herriott's Point

Aurora Locations in Dover and Strathblane

Scott Point

Memorial Park and Information Bay

The Old Brick Kiln

Dover public jetty

CHASING AURORA AUSTRALIS

Dover Beach

Roaring Bay Beach

Kent Beach

Little Roaring Bay Beach

Aurora Locations in Kettering, Port Huon, Petcheys Bay, Eggs and Bacon Bay, Gordon, and Woodbridge

CHASING AURORA AUSTRALIS

Kermandie Boardwalk

Brabazon Point

Drip Beach

Mickeys Beach

Randalls Bay

Pickup Beach

Ninepin Point Marine Reserve

Gordon Boat Ramp

Woodbridge Jetty

Trial Bay Boat Ramp

Aurora Locations in Bruny Island

Cape Bruny Lighthouse

Cape Bruny Lookout

Bruny Island Lighthouse Carpark

Butlers Beach

CHASING AURORA AUSTRALIS

East Cloudy Head

Conleys Beach

Cemetery Beach

Two Tree Point

Penguin View

Blighs Rocks

The Arch

Miles Beach

Variety Bay Pilot Station

Trumpeter Rd

Whaymans Rd

Aurora Locations in Tinderbox, Howden, and Bonnet Hill

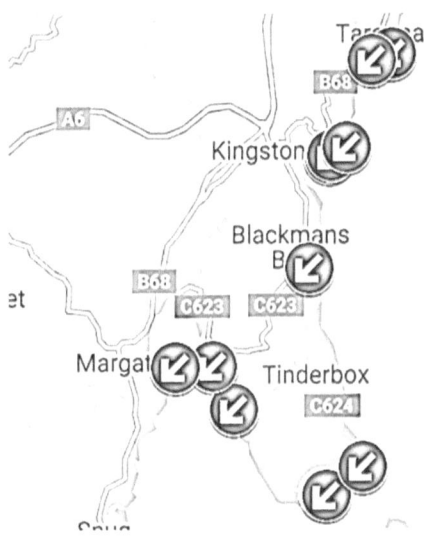

Tinderbox Beach

Howden Boat Ramp

Tinderbox Boat Ramp

Blackmans Bay Beach

Pierson's Point Light

Kingston Dog Beach

CHASING AURORA AUSTRALIS

Tyndall Beach

Hinsby Beach

Cliff view point

Taroona Beach

Aurora Locations in Hobart, Tranmere, Rosny, Seven Mile Beach, Penna, and Wellington Park

Pindos Park

Surf Road Plane Watching Area

Rosny Hill Lookout

Penna Beach

Post Master General Tower

Lattice Tower

Parking Mount Wellington

Mount Wellington North East Viewing Platform

South West Viewing Platform

Aurora Locations in Dodges Ferry, Carlton, Primrose Sands, Marion Bay, and Bream Creek

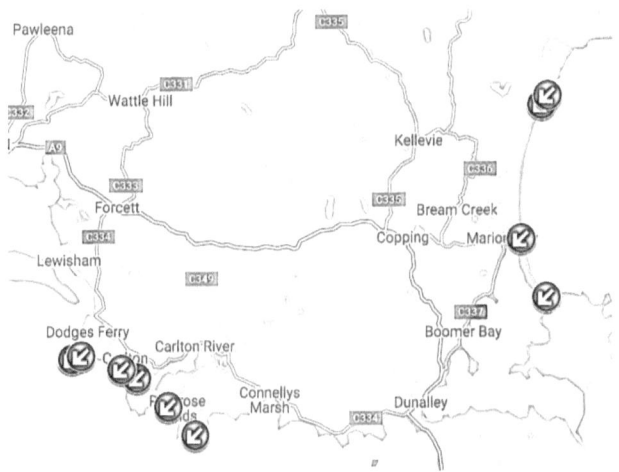

Rocky the Whale Lookout

Spectacle Head - National Whale Trail

Park Beach

Carlton Beach

Primrose Sands Beach

Gypsy Bay Boat Ramp

Marion Beach

Marion Bay Viewing Platform

Eagles Beach

Shelly beach

Aurora Locations in Cape Raoul, Port Arthur, Cape Pillar, White Beach, Nubeena, Port Arthur, Fortescue, and Eaglehawk Neck

Cape Raoul Viewing Point

Seal Rock Lookout

The Gap

Cape Raoul Lookout

Shipstern Bluff

Mount Brown

CHASING AURORA AUSTRALIS

Crescent Bay Beach

Maingon Bay Lookout

Safety Cove beach

The Blade

Wedge Bay

Roaring Beach

Frying Pan Point

Cape Hauy

Waterfall bay lookout

Pirates Bay Beach

Tessellated Pavement

Tasman Bay National Park Lookout

Aurora Locations in Maria Island and Orford

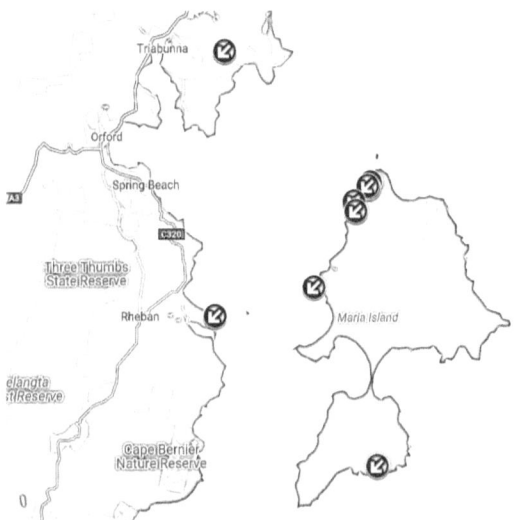

Haunted Bay

Rheban Beach

Return Point

Rutherford Beach

Across from
Painted Cliffs

Hopground Beach

Maria Island Ferry Terminal	Banwell Beach

Aurora Locations in Freycinet, Coles Bay, Dolphin Sands, and Swansea

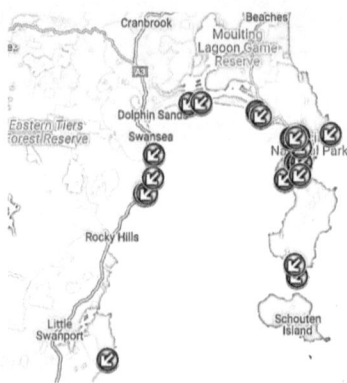

Spiky Bridge	Coswell Beach

Cressy Beach	9 Mile Beach Access

Nine Mile Beach

Honeymoon Bay

Sandpiper Beach

Coles Bay Lookout

Foreshore Walk

Wineglass Bay Lookout

Coles Bay Lookout

Mount Amos Lookout

Coles Bay Boat Ramp

Hazards Beach

Richardsons Beach

Wineglass Bay

CHASING AURORA AUSTRALIS

Bryans Beach

Passage Beach

Aurora Locations in Ross and Oatlands

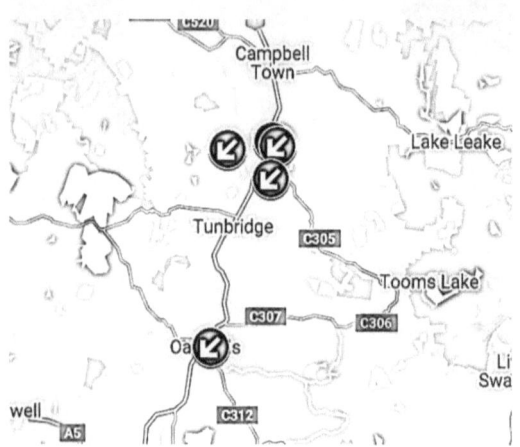

Public Toilet (Oatlands)

Auburn Rd

Mona Vale Rd

Ross Pioneer cemetery

Ross Anglican Cemetery

Ross Bridge

Aurora Locations in Ouse, Bothwell, Hamilton, Karanja, Macquarie Plains, New Norfolk, and Campania

Tor Hill Rd

Hollow Tree Rd

Guilford

Mount Rd

Hamilton Plains Rd

Cawthorns Ln

Anm Karanja Fire Station

Pulpit Rock Lookout

Coal River Bridge

Aurora Locations in Lake Pedder, Southwest, and Florentine

Serpentine Dam

Pedder Lake Lookout

Highest Point On Road

Aurora Locations in Cape Sorell, Strahan, and Gormanston

Discovery Beach

Charleys Beach

CHASING AURORA AUSTRALIS

Grandfathers Beach

Ocean Beach Lookout

Cape Sorell Lighthouse

Iron Blow Lookout

Aurora Locations in Central Plateau and Liawenee

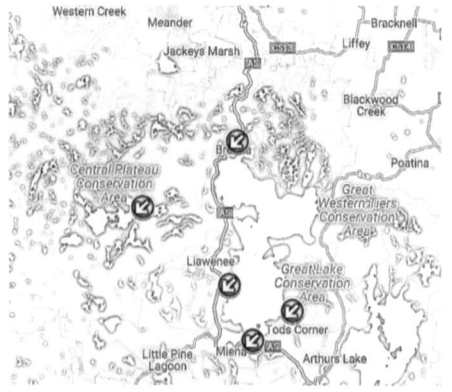

Public toilet (Central Plateau)

Great lakes lookout

Great Lake point 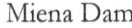 Miena Dam

Aurora Locations in Bicheno and Chain of Lagoons

Bicheno Blowhole

Seymour Beach

Picaninny point

Aurora Locations in Nunamara, Deddington, Ben Lomond, and Mangana

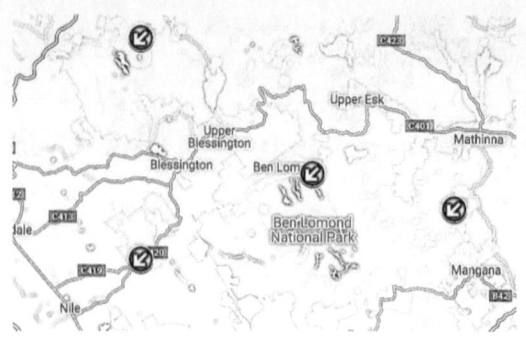

Mount Barrow lookout

Jacob's Ladder

Deddington Rd

East Tower Lookout

CHASING AURORA AUSTRALIS

Aurora Locations in Akaroa, Binalong Bay, The Gardens, Ansons Bay, and Eddystone

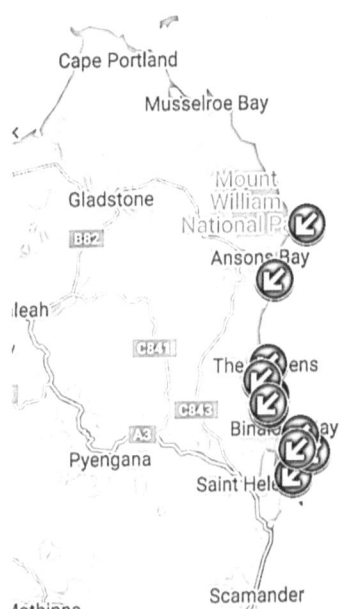

Maurouard Beach

Beerbarrel Beach

Peron Dunes

Humbug Point Nature Recreation Area

CHASING AURORA AUSTRALIS

Grants Point

Swimcart Beach

Cosy Corner North

Orange Rock

Sloop Rock Lookout

Taylors Beach

Suicide Beach

Policemans Point

Eddystone Point Lighthouse

Aurora Locations in Bridport

Adams Beach

Mermaids Pool

Aurora Locations in Launceston, Trevallyn, Rosevears, and Hillwood

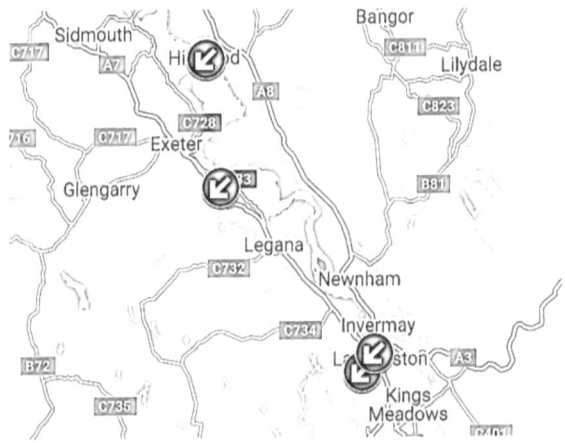

Alexandra Suspension Bridge

Bradys Lookout State Reserve

Tamar River

Hillwood Pontoon

Aurora Locations in Low Head

Low Head Breakwater

Lagoon Beach

CHASING AURORA AUSTRALIS

Aurora Locations in Devonport

Braddons Lookout

Aurora Locations in Cradle Mountain, Tullah, and Liena

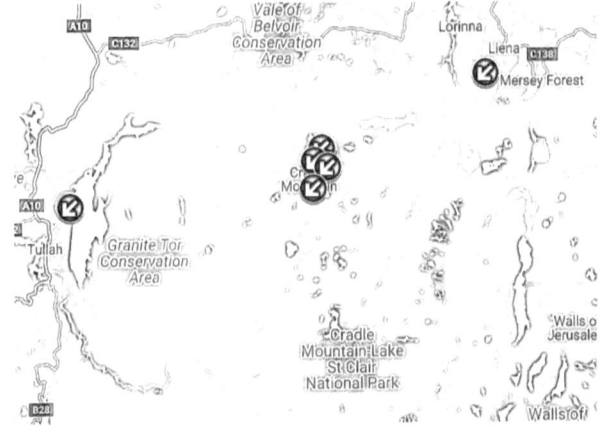

Mackintosh Dam

Dove Lake Boatshed

Cradle Mountain Summit

Cradle365 Photo Holder

Hansons Peak

Glacier Rock

Marions Lookout

Dove Lake Carpark

Lemonthyme Road Scenic Lookout

CHASING AURORA AUSTRALIS

Aurora Locations in West Coast, Temma, Arthur River, Marrawah, Montagu, Irishtown, Stanley, and Rocky Cape

Sandy Cape (Tas) Lighthouse

Sandy Cape Beach

Start of Sandy Cape Track (North)

Lady Kathleen Beach

Arthur Beach

Edge Of the World

CHASING AURORA AUSTRALIS

Bluff Hill Point

Lighthouse Beach

Bens Hill Rd

Monson Rd

Irishtown General Cemetery

Faheys Ln

Highfield Lookout

Fisherman's Wharf Lookout

Stanley jetty

Trethewies Lookout

Pinmatik - Lutruwita

Aurora Locations in King Island

Stokes Point Lighthouse

Seal Wall Gulchway bay

Broken Arm Beach

Grassy Penguin Colony

Mutton bird /
Short Tailed Shearwaters
Colony

CHASING AURORA AUSTRALIS

Seal Rocks Lookout

Copper Head Trail / Lookout

Cataraqui Gravesite Memorial

Sandfly Beach

Netherby Point

British Admiral Beach

Currie Lighthouse

Porky Beach

Whistler Point

CHASING AURORA AUSTRALIS

Aurora Locations in Flinders Island

Freds Beach

Lady Barron Pier

Watering Beach

Yellow Beaches

13
PRIME AURORA LOCATIONS - VIC

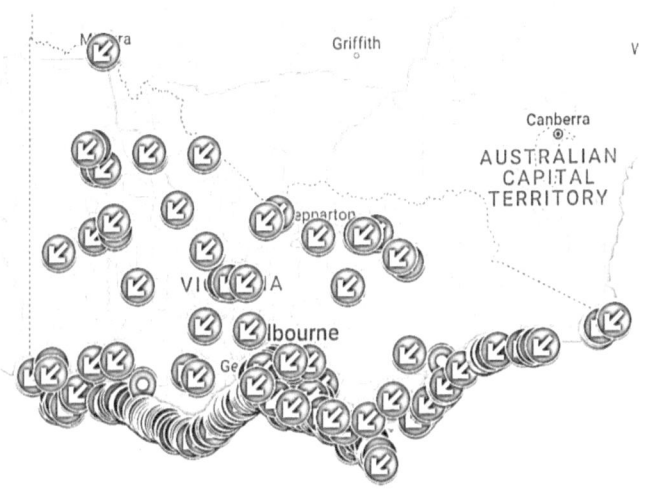

QR Code for 370+ VIC Aurora locations

Aurora Locations in Nelson, Drik Drik, and Dartmoor

Discovery Bay bird observatory

Jones lookout

Punt Hill Lookout

Korrey Smith Hill Scenic lookout

Aurora Locations in Cape Bridgewater, Portland West, Allestree, and Narrawong

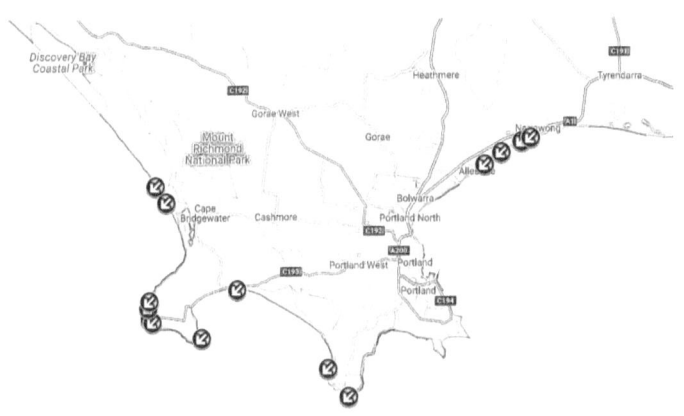

Discovery Bay Coastal Park

Black's Beach

The Green Pools

Limestone & Basalt Lookout

Bridgewater Blowholes

Petrified Forest

CHASING AURORA AUSTRALIS

Seal Colony Viewing Platform

Bishops Rock

Discovery Bay Marine National Park

Cape Nelson Lighthouse

Convincing Ground

Coast road east

Surrey River Public toilet

Aurora Locations in Byaduk and Penshurst

Harmans Valley Lookout

Mt Rouse Lookout

Mount Rouse

Mount Rouse Reserve

Mount Rouse

Aurora Locations in Port Fairy, Yambuk, Killarney, and Tower Hill

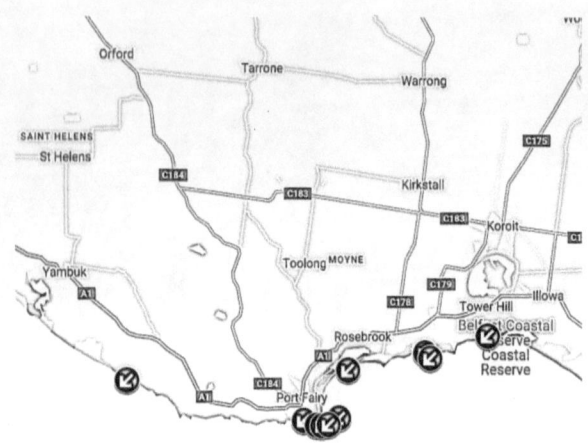

The Crags

Southcombe Beach

The Passage

Griffiths Island Reserve Track

Griffiths Island Reserve

Port Fairy Lighthouse

East Beach

Killarney Beach

Killarney Boat Ramp

Belfast Coastal Reserve

Aurora Locations in Warrnambool and Allansford

Thunder Point

Pickering Point Lookout

Pickering Point

Stingray Bay

Old aquariums at Warrnambool Harbour

McGennans Beach

Surf Club Beach

Surfside Beach

The Flume Beach

The Flume Beach (East)

Granny's Grave Beach

Warrnambool Beach Lookout

Moyjil / Point Ritchie

Logans Beach Whale Nursery

Logans Beach Whale Watching Platform

Rifle Range Lookout

Aurora Locations in Peterborough, Princetown, Nirranda South, Nullawarre, and Mepunga

Childers Cove

Sandy Bay beach

Buttress Point

The Cove

Flaxmans Hill Car Park

Flaxmans Hill

Point Riley

The Great Ship

Bay Of Islands

Halladale Point

Sancho Lookout

Port Campbell

James Irvine Monument

The Grotto

London Bridge

Sunset lookout

The Point

Prady's Lookout

Marcus point

The Bakers Oven

The Razorback Lookout

Twelve Apostles Viewpoint

Castle Rock

CHASING AURORA AUSTRALIS

Gibson Beach

Gibson Steps

Aurora Locations in Hordern Vale, Glenaire, Johanna, and Gellibrand Lower

Princetown Beach

Rivernook Beach

CHASING AURORA AUSTRALIS

Wreck Beach

Johanna Beach

The Gables

Castle Cove Lookout

Milanesia Beach

Aire River Beach

Station Beach

Aurora Locations in Apollo Bay, Wongarra, Sugarloaf, Skenes Creek, and Marengo

Shelly Beach

Apollo Bay Breakwater

Marker Beacon Lookout

Marriner's Lookout

Cunningham point

Biddles Beach

Skenes Creek Beach

Sugarloaf Beach

Cape Patton Lookout

Aurora Locations in Lismore and Cundare North

Mckechnies Rd

Cundare Pools

Aurora Locations in Dimboola, Lake Lonsdale, Peronne, Wallup, and Cannum

Lake Lonsdale

Sisters Hill lookout

Pink Lake

Moloneys Rd

Aubrey Rd

Aurora Locations in Lake Tyrrell, Yaapeet, Big Desert, Lake Boga, and Merbein

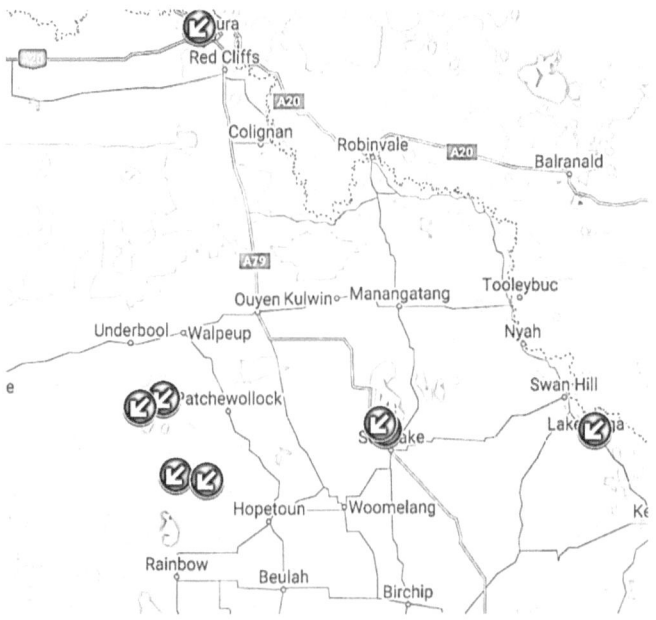

Western Lookout Dune   O'Sullivan's Lookout

Eastern Lookout   Kelly's Lookout

Lake Tyrrell Sunrise view

Lake Boga Camp Ground
501-523

Lake Tyrrell Viewing Platform

Merbein Lookout

Aurora Locations in Echuca, Wycheproof, Brenanah, Baringhup, Maldon, Harcourt North, and Bamawm

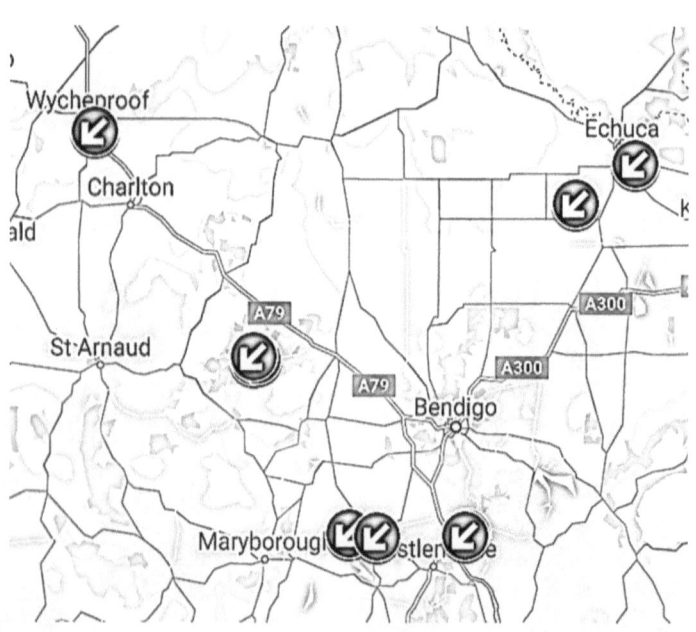

Gretgrix Rd

Melville Caves Lookout

Southern Lookout

McLeods Lookout

Cairn Curran Weir

Unnamed Road, Baringhup

Mount Tarrengower Lookout

Shepherd's Flat Lookout

Lang's Lookout

Bamawm Rd

Benson Rd

Aurora Locations in Ballarat

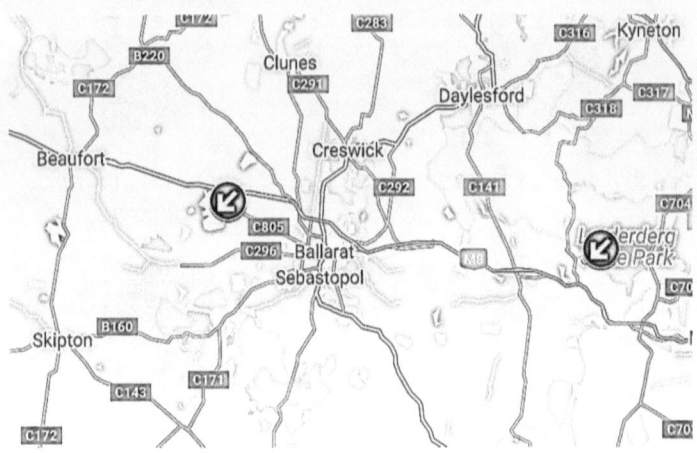

Lake Burrumbeet   Mt Blackwood Summit

Aurora Locations in Wangaratta, Kialla, Chesney Vale, Winton North, and Laceby

Mitchell Rd

Greens Hill Walk

Winton Wetlands

Winton Wetlands CFA Water Tank

Brian Higgins Dr

Aurora Locations in Mount Buffalo and Buffalo River

Lake Buffalo

The Horn Lookout

The Horn Picnic Area

Aurora Locations in Bonnie Doon

Kennedys Point

Aurora Locations in Traralgon, Mount Tassie and Maffra West Upper

Mount Tassie Lookout

Pearsons Point Lookout

CHASING AURORA AUSTRALIS

Aurora Locations in Great Ocean Rd, Separation Creek, Lorne, Big Hill, Eastern View, and Moggs Creek

Artillery Rocks

St Georges River lookout

Mount Defiance Lookout

Teddy's Lookout

Cumberland River Beach

Jump Rock

Big Hill

Devil's Elbow

Sprout Creek

Eastern View 3

Eastern View 2

Eastern View

Moggs Creek beach

Aurora Locations in Anglesea and Great Ocean Road

Sentinel Rock

Urquhart Bluff Lookout

Loutit Bay Lookout

Urquhart Bluff

Split Point Lookout

Car Park Anglesea

Eagle Rock Lookout

Land's End Lookout

Guvvos Beach

Reef Lookout

O'Donohues Beach

Point Roadknight Beach Carpark

Point Roadknight Lookout

Aurora Locations in Bells Beach, Torquay and Jan Juc

Point Addis Marine National Park

Point Addis Boardwalk

Hingu Point

Point Addis Beach

CHASING AURORA AUSTRALIS

Point Addis Beach Lookout

Bells Beach

Addiscot Beach

Winkipop

Jarosite Launch

Bells Beach Lookout

Southside Beach

Lookout (Bells Beach)

Southside Carpark

Bird Rock Lookout

Bells Beach Lookout Platform

Lookout (Jan Juc)

Little Bird Rock Lookout

Rocky Point Lookout

Harry's Lookout

The Three Posts of Sign

Jan Juc Beach

Sundial

Aurora Locations in Torquay, Breamlea, and Connewarre

Whites Beach

Callenas Beach

CHASING AURORA AUSTRALIS

Point Impossible Beach

Point Impossible Car Park

Breamlea Victoria

Buckley's Bay Beach

Bancoora beach lookout

Bancoora Beach

Black Rocks

Aurora Locations in Barwon Heads, Ocean Grove, Queenscliff, Connewarre, Leopold, St Leonards, and Point Lonsdale

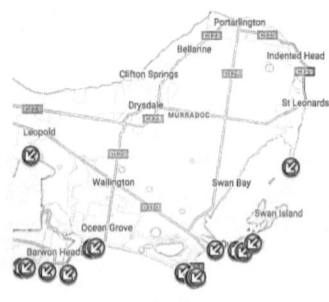

Thirteenth Beach

Boings Thirteenth Beach

Barwon Heads 13th Beach

Barwon Heads Bluff

The Lookout
(Ocean Grove)

Ocean Grove Beach

Lake Connewarre Lookout

Two Bays Lookout

Queenscliff South Pier

Shortland Bluff

Queenscliff White
Lighthouse

Queenscliff Lookout

CHASING AURORA AUSTRALIS

Queenscliff Beach

Point Lonsdale Lighthouse

Point Lonsdale Dog Beach

Hardie Lookout

Point Lonsdale Jetty

Point Lonsdale Back Beach Base

Aurora Locations in Avalon and Point Wilson

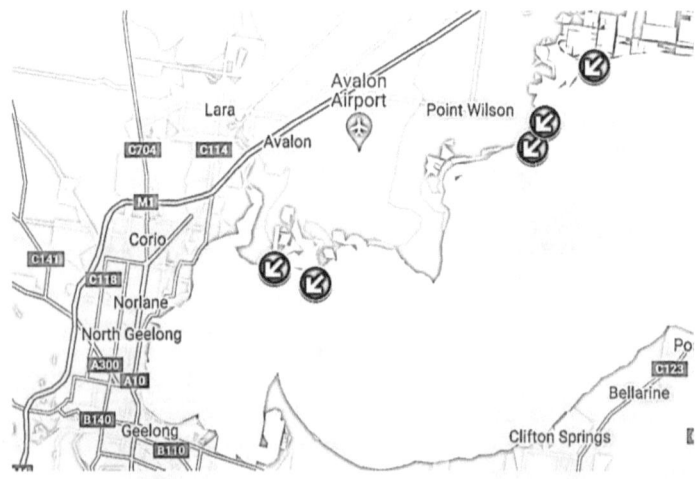

Avalon Beach

Point Wilson Boat Ramp

Point Lillias

Little River Bird Hide

Kirk Point

Aurora Locations in Werribee, Tarneit, Hoppers Crossing, Wyndham Vale, and Point Cook

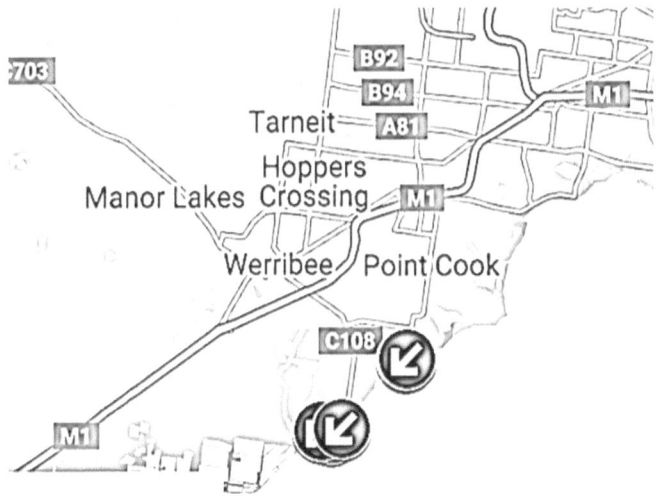

Werribee South Foreshore

Werribee South Beach

East Beach - Werribee South

Beach Walkway

Campbells Cove Beach

Aurora Locations in Melbourne, Brighton, Black Rock, Beaumaris, Dandenong, and Lysterfield

Green Point

Red Bluff Lookout

Ricketts Point Marine Sanctuary

Southernmost Point Of City of Bayside

Trig Point Lookout

Aurora Locations in Blind Bight, Tooradin, and Koo Wee Rup

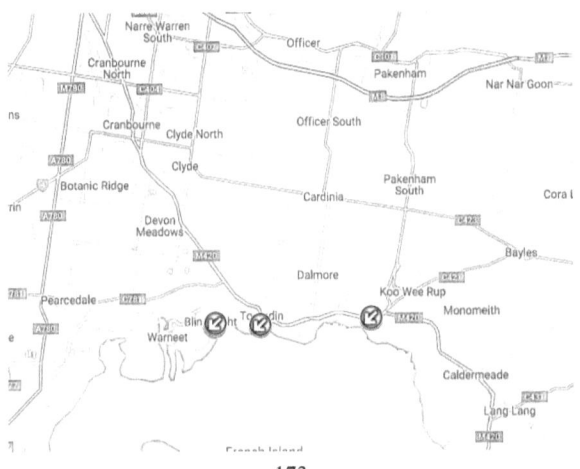

Blind Bight Observation Deck

Tooradin Boat Ramp

Blind Bight Boat Ramp

Koo Wee Rup Observation Tower

Aurora Locations in Portsea, Sorrento, Blairgowrie, and Rye

Cheviot West Beach Lookout

Monash Light Lookout

Eagles Nest

London Bridge Lookout

CHASING AURORA AUSTRALIS

Portsea Surf Beach

Bay of Islands

Back Beach

Jubilee Point

Sphinx Rock

Koonya Beach

Coppins Lookout

Spray Point

Sorrento Ocean Beach

Montforts Beach

St Pauls Beach

Pearses Beach

CHASING AURORA AUSTRALIS

Dimmicks Beach

Lizard Head Rock

Aurora Locations in St Andrews Beach, Fingal, Cape Schanck, and Flinders

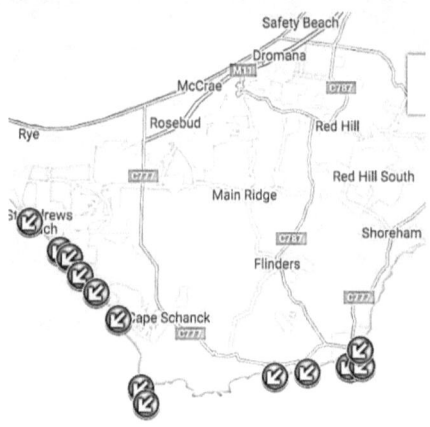

Rye Ocean Beach

St Andrews Beach (II)

St Andrews Beach (I)

Boag Rocks

Gunnamatta Ocean Beach

Gunnamatta Beach

Cape Schanck Lighthouse

Pulpit Rock

Cairn Beach

Flinders Blowhole

Ocean Beach

Mushroom Reef Marine Sanctuary Viewing Platform

West Head Lookout

Flinders Ocean Lookout

Aurora Locations in Point Leo, Western Port Bay, Balnarring Beach, and Somers

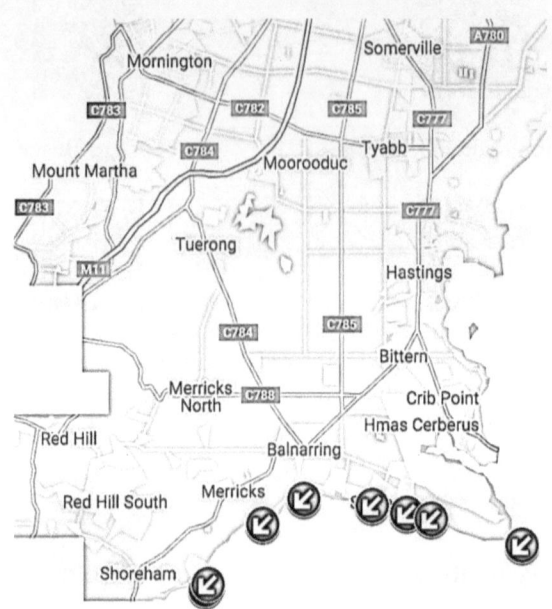

Deep rockpool

'Crunchie Point' Lookout

Merricks Beach Foreshore Reserve

Balnarring Beach

Somers Beach

Western Park Beach

South Beach

Sandy Point

Aurora Locations in French Island

Tankerton Pier

The Pinnacles Lookout

French Island Barge

Aurora Locations in Phillip Island

Seal Rock Lookout

Shipwreck SS Speke

The Nobbies View Point

Berrys Beach

Southpoint Lookout

Berry Beach

South Coast Lookout

Redcliff Head

CHASING AURORA AUSTRALIS

Red Bluff Lookout

Storm Bay Lookout

Pyramid Rock Lookout

Smiths Beach

Surfies Point

Surf Beach Viewing Point

Forest Caves Beach

Forrest Caves

The Colonnades

Anzacs Beach

Woolamai Surf Beach (I)

Woolamai Surf Beach (II)

Magiclands Steps

Cape Woolamai Beacon

Pinnacles Lookout

Gull Island Lookout

Aurora Locations in San Remo and Kilcunda

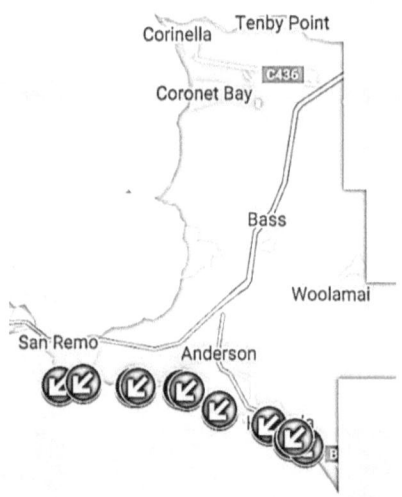

Griffith Point

Cadillac Canyon

Punchbowl Rocks Beach Lookout

Punchbowl Rocks Beach

Half Moon Bay

Throne Rock Beach

Sandy Waterhole Beach

Shelley Beach

Elephant Rock

Kilcunda Trestle Railway Bridge

Kilcunda Surf Beach

CHASING AURORA AUSTRALIS

Aurora Locations in Inverloch, Wonthaggi, Cape Paterson, and Venus Bay

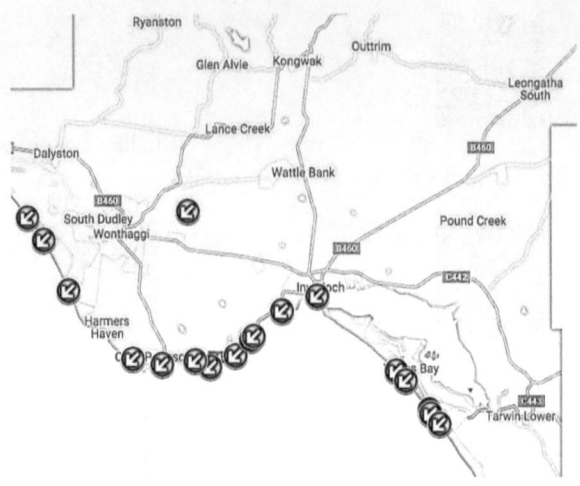

Williamson's Beach

Cutlers Beach

Baxter Beach

F Break beach

Kirrak Rd

Cape Paterson Rock Pool

CHASING AURORA AUSTRALIS

The Oaks	Anderson's Inlet
Twin Reefs Car Park	No 5 Beach
Eagles Nest	No 4 Beach
The Caves Beach	No 3 Beach
Flat Rocks- Dinosaur Dreaming Fossil Site	No 2 Beach
Inverloch Surf Beach	Venus Bay

Aurora Locations in Wilsons Promontory, Foster, Tarwin Lower, Waratah Bay, and Sandy Point

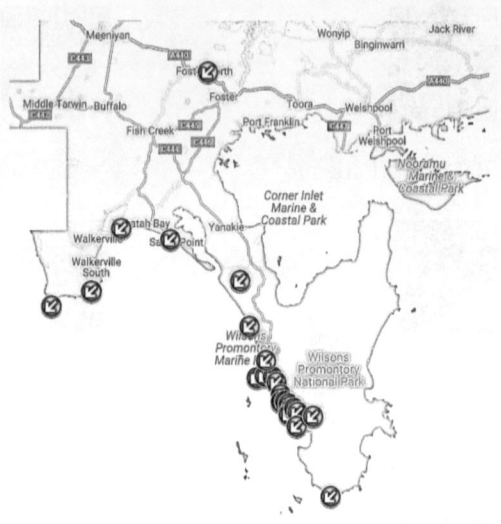

Foster North Lookout

Waratah Bay beach

Cape Liptrap Lighthouse

Dunes of the Big Drift

Maitland Beach

Ned Neale's Lookout

CHASING AURORA AUSTRALIS

Norman Beach

Norman Point Lookout

Mount Oberon Summit

South Point

Aurora Locations in Mcloughlins Beach, McGauran Beach, and Glomar Beach

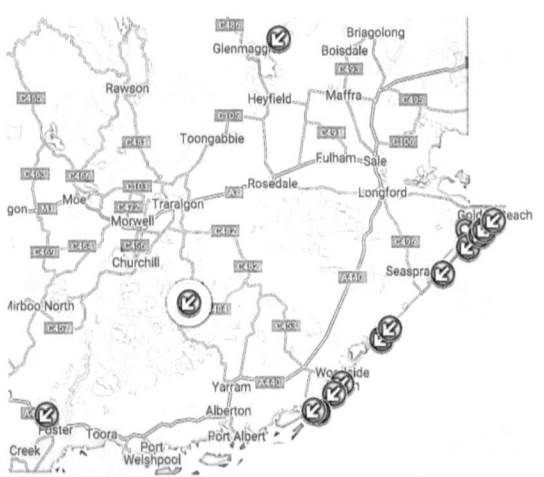

Mcloughlin's Beach Jetty

Mcloughlins Beach

Reeves Beach

Woodside Beach

McGauran Beach

McGaurans Beach free campground

Glomar Beach

Beach Access, Glomar Beach

Flamingo Beach

The Wreck Beach

Delray Beach

Ninety Mile Beach

CHASING AURORA AUSTRALIS

Aurora Locations in Lakes Entrance, Ocean Grange, Nyerimilang, Lake Tyers Beach, Cape Conran, and Bemm River

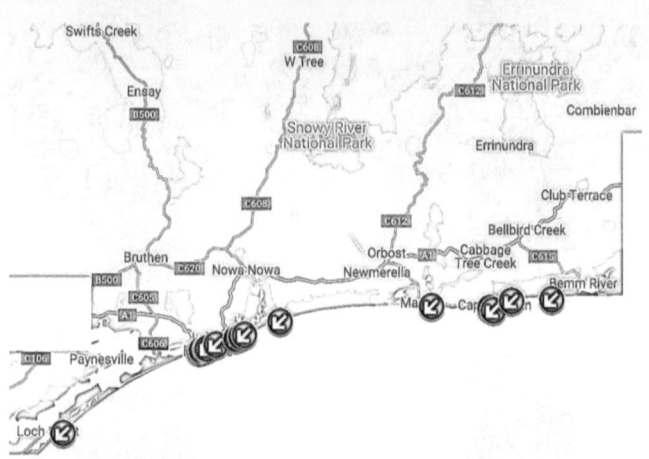

Ninety Mile Beach Lookout

Lakes Entrance Lookout

Drew's Front Beach

Sand Transfer Pipe

Flagstaff Lookout

Lakes Entrance Beach

Eastern Beach

Red Bluff Surfing Beach

Beacon Reserve Viewing Platform

Lake Tyers Beach

Pettmans Beach

Mots Beach

Jacksons Beach

Salmon Rocks

Yeerung River Outlet

Pearl Point

Aurora Locations in Mallacoota

Secret Beach Lookout

Davis Creek Beach

Quarry Beach

Betka Beach

Geology Point Victoria

Easternmost point of Victoria

14
PRIME AURORA
LOCATIONS - SA

QR Code for 90+ SA Aurora locations

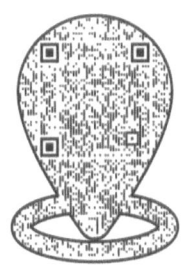

Aurora Locations in Elliston, Bramfield, Kiana, Coulta, Coffin Bay, Sleaford, Sleaford, and Lincoln National Park

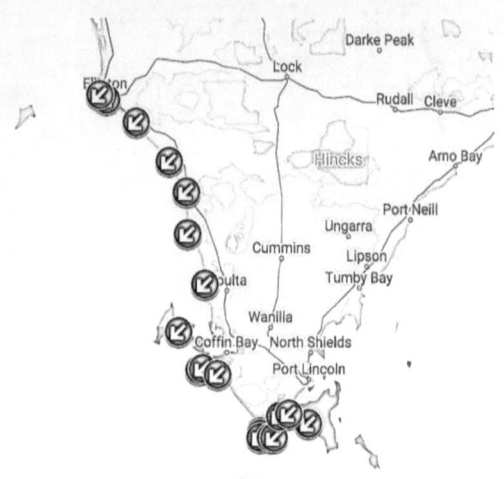

Elliston Mara Sculpture on the Cliffs

Little Bay

Locks Well Beach

Sheringa Beach

Cummings monument lookout

Picnic Beach

Red Banks Beach

Greenly Beach

Theakstone Crevasse

Sensation Beach

Blowhole & Baleen Rockpool

Almonta Beach

Blacks Lookout

Golden Island Lookout

Cape Wiles

Gunya Beach

Lone Pine Lookout

Tinah Beach

West Wanna lookout

Aurora Locations in Inneston, Marion Bay, Foul Bay, Port Moorowie, and Honiton

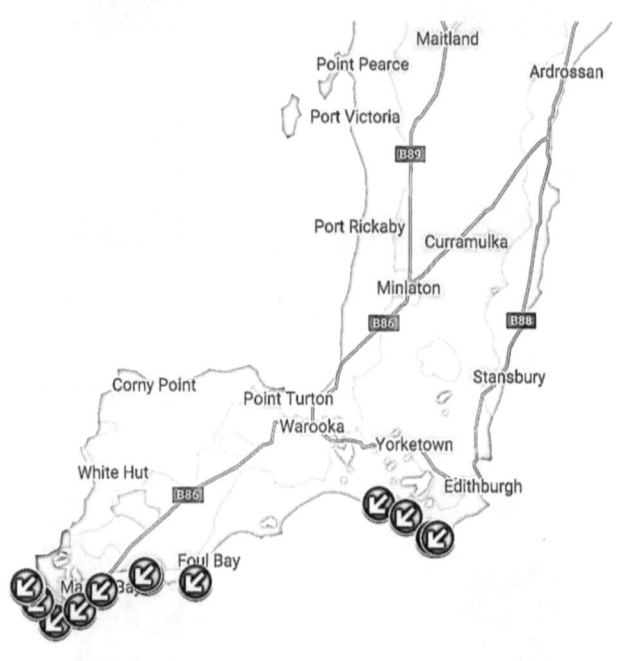

West Cape Lighthouse

West Cape Lookout

Ethel Wreck Beach Lookout

Cape Spencer Lighthouse

Gulawulgawi Ngunda Nhagu - Cape Spencer Lookout

Willyama beach

Ganarabba

Meehan Hill Lookout

Kangaroo Island Lookout

Mceacherns Beach

Kemp Bay

Troubridge Point lighthouse

Troubridge Hill Aquatic Reserve

Aurora Locations in Kangaroo Island

Weirs Lookout

Hanson Bay Beach

Remarkable Rocks Lookout

Vivonne Bay Rock Pool

Remarkable Rocks

Bales Beach

Pennington Bay Beach
Access Path

Sea Dragon Rock

Cape Willoughby
Lighthouse Carpark

Aurora Locations in Encounter Bay, Victor Harbor, Carrickalinga, Deep Creek, Tunkalilla, Waitpinga, Chiton, Port Elliot, and Hindmarsh Island

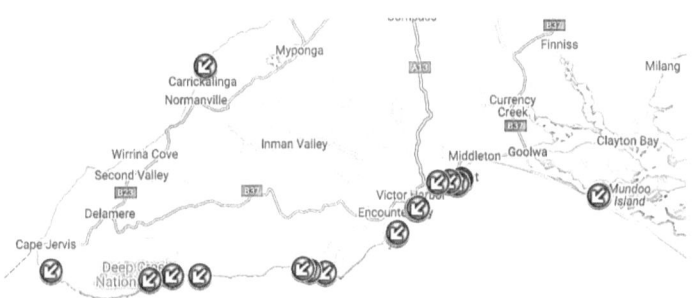

Carrickalinga Point
Lookout

Fishery Beach

CHASING AURORA AUSTRALIS

Tapanappa Lookout

Petrel Cove Beach

Boat Harbor Beach

The Bluff, Encounter Bay

Tunkalilla Beach

View point (Victor Harbor)

Parsons Beach

Granite Island Recreation Park

Muhan Aurora Viewpoint

Chiton Beach

Waitpinga Beach

CHASING AURORA AUSTRALIS

Lookout (Port Elliot)

Commodore Point

Freemans Knob

Sugars Beach

Aurora Locations in Adelaide, Hallett Cove, Onkaparinga Hills, Palmer, Eden Valley, and Bethany

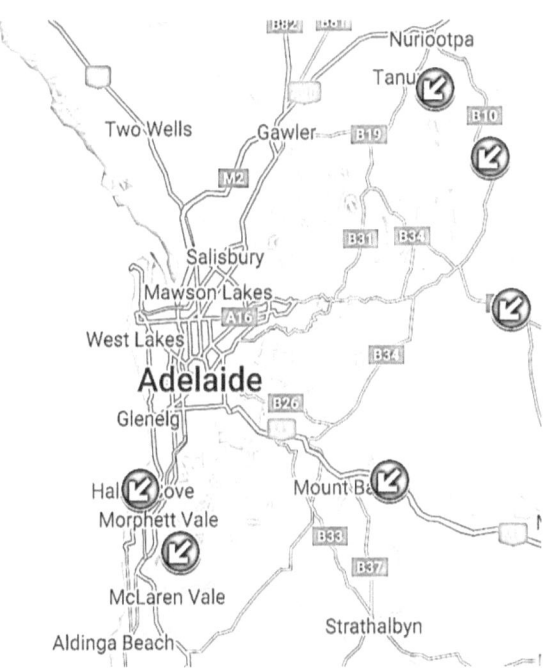

Hallett Cove Boardwalk

Scenic View Point Palmer Lookout

Punchbowl Lookout and Trails

Eden Valley Lookout

Mt Barker Summit Lookout

Mengler Hill Lookout

Aurora Locations in Mount Gambier, Canunda, Carpenter Rocks, Cape Douglas, Port Macdonnell, Eight Mile Creek, Coorong, Nora Creina, and Beachport

CHASING AURORA AUSTRALIS

Geltwood Beach

Finger point beach

Admella Beach

Finger Point lookout

Cape Banks Lighthouse

South Australia's Southern Most Point

Bucks Bay Beach

Shelly Beach

Douglas Point

Ian Mitchener Birdhide

Shelly Beach Lookout

Brown Bay Freedom Camping

CHASING AURORA AUSTRALIS

Jack Point Observatory Deck

Long Beach

Photo Point lookout

Little Dip Beach

Cowrie Island

Post Office Rock

Beachport View Point

Beachport Boat Ramp

Cowrie Beach

Cape Buffon Carpark

Viewing platform
(Canunda)

Cullen Bay Lookout

Mcintyre Beach

CHASING AURORA AUSTRALIS

15
PRIME AURORA
LOCATIONS - WA

QR Code for 140+ WA Aurora locations

Aurora Locations in Perth, Bickley, Flint, York, and Birchmont

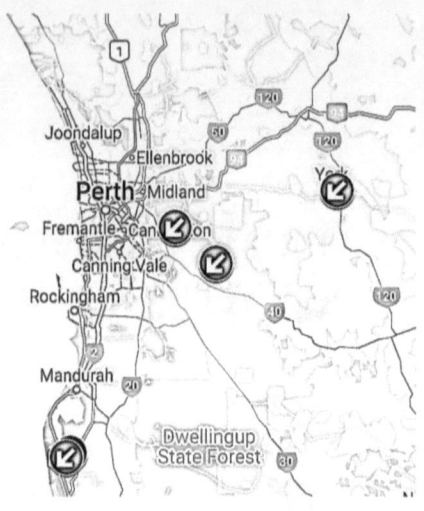

Perth Observatory

Mount Brown Lookout

Mount Dale Lookout

Herron Point Boat Ramp & Carpark

CHASING AURORA AUSTRALIS

Aurora Locations in Naturaliste, Busselton, Injidup, Redgate, Boranup, Hamelin Bay, Deepdene, Deepdene, Augusta, and Leeuwin

Cape Naturaliste

Fede spot

Wilanup Lookout

Sugarloaf Rock

CHASING AURORA AUSTRALIS

Three Bears

Canal Rocks

Injidup Point

Redgate Beach

Car Park Boranup

Car Park Boranup (Second Location)

South Beach Car Park

Car Park Hooley Rd

Boranup Rocks

Boranup Cliffs Lookout

Hamelin Bay Observation Deck

Knobby Head

Car Park Deepdene

Cosy Corner Beach

Deepdene Beach

Hillview Road Lookout

Leeuwin Lookout
(Salt Point)

Flinder's bay
rocky beach

Granny's Pool

Flinders Bay Jetty

Aurora Locations in Lake Jasper, Yeagarup, and Windy Harbour

Surfers Cove

Jasper Beach

Donnelly Rivermouth

Yeagarup Dunes

Yeagarup Beach

Malimup Beach

Tookulup Lookout

Cathedral Rock Beach

The Window

Boat Ramp

Point d'Entrecasteaux

Coodamurrup Beach

Aurora Locations in Broke, Nornalup, Peaceful Bay, Parryville, Denmark, William Bay, Ocean Beach, and Nullaki

Cliffy Head	Shelly Beach
Geezly Beach	Conspicuous Cliff
Mandalay Beach	Peaceful Bay
Hush Hush Beach	Quarram Beach
Circus Beach	Eagles Nest
Bellanger Beach	Hillier Beach

CHASING AURORA AUSTRALIS

Greens Pool

Central beach

Madfish Bay Lookout

Back Beach

Madfish Bay

Sinker Bay

Waterfall Beach

Black Hole Rock

Lights Beach Clothing Optional Area

Anvil Beach

Lights Beach

Anvil Beach Lookout

Aurora Locations in Albany, West Cape Howe, Kronkup, Elleker, Sandpatch, Torndirrup, Kalgan, Nanarup, Cheynes, and Green Range

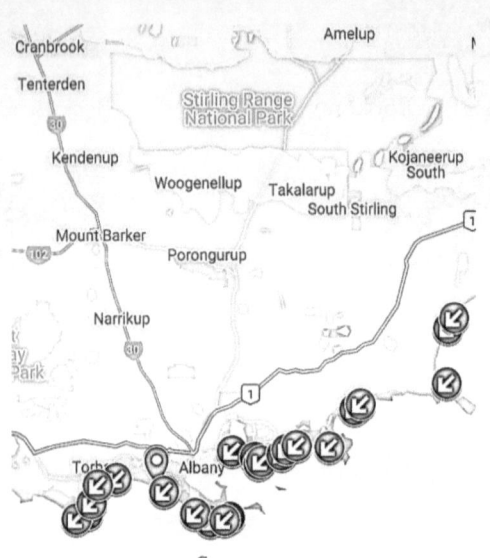

Golden Gate Beach

Dingo Beach

Shelley Beach Lookout

Perkins Beach

Mutton Bird Beach Lookout

Cave Point Light House

Sand Patches

Blowholes

Whale Watching Platform

Jimmy Newell's Harbour Lookout

Albany Wind Farm

Emu Beach

Sharp Point Lookout

Gull Rock Beach

CHASING AURORA AUSTRALIS

Ledge Point

Bettys Beach

Skippy Reef Beach

Normans Beach

Ben Dearg Beach

Cheynes Bay Lookout

Nanarup Beach

Cheyne Beach

Sinker Reef

Hassell Beach

Aurora Locations in Bremer Bay, Fitzgerald River National Park, Hopetoun, and Jerdacuttup

Pallinup Beach

Banky Beach

Foster Beach

Peppermint Beach

Dillon Beach

Trigelow Beach

CHASING AURORA AUSTRALIS

Point Ann Fish Hole

Point Ann

Whalebone Beach

West Beach

Mylies Beach

East Mileys

Barrens Beach

Four Mile Beach

Culham Beach

Hopetoun Jetty

Hopetoun Beach

2 Mile Beach

12 Mile Beach

Aurora Locations in Esperance, Bandy Creek, Cape Le Grand, Howick, Coomalbidgup, Dalyup, West Beach, and Castletown

Wylie Head Beach

Wylie Bay Rock

Hellfire Bay

Thistle Cove

CHASING AURORA AUSTRALIS

| Lucky Bay | Butty Head Beach |

| Drapala Beach | 13 Mile Beach |

| Kennedy Beach | 11 Mile Beach |

| Munglinup Beach | Eleven Mile Lagoon |

| Skippy Rock | Ten Mile Lagoon |

| Quagi Beach | Nine mile lagoon |

Observatory Beach

Esperance Great Ocean Drive

Observatory Point

Fourth Beach

Twilight Beach Lookout

Blue Haven Rock

Lovers Cove

West Beach

Twilight Beach

Rotary Lookout

Salmon Beach

Lover's Beach lookout

CHASING AURORA AUSTRALIS

Dempster Head

Castletown Beach

16
PRIME AURORA LOCATIONS - ACT

QR Code for 10+ ACT Aurora locations

Historic Waterholes Hut

Historic Brayshaws Homestead

Tor Viewpoint

Hospital Hill Lookout

Lambrigg's Lookout

Big Monks Summit

Red Rock Gorge Lookout

Shepherds Lookout

Dairy Farmers Hill Lookout

Black Mountain Lookout

Mount Ainslie Lookout

17
PRIME AURORA LOCATIONS - NSW

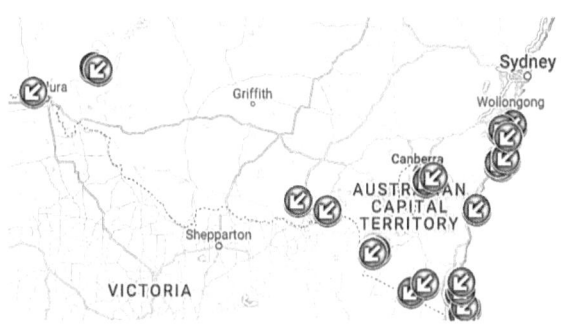

QR Code for 40+ NSW Aurora locations

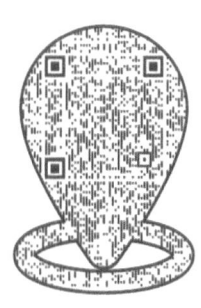

Aurora Locations in Wentworth and Mungo National Park

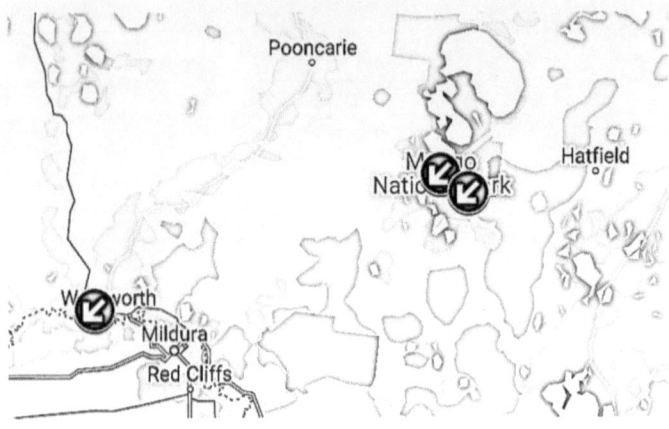

Perry Sandhills Public Toilets

Mungo lookout

Mungo National Park

Aurora Locations in Albury, Walla Walla and Wantagong

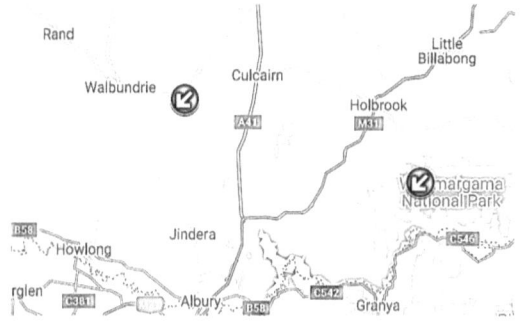

Morgan's Lookout

Norths Lookout

Aurora Locations in Kosciuszko, Geehi, and Charlotte Pass

Cootapatamba Lookout

Mount Stilwell Walk

Kosciuszko lookout

Charlotte Pass

Charlotte Pass lookout

Aurora Locations in Delegate, Bombala, Nadgee, Wonboyn, Green Cape, Eden, and Merimbula

Delegate Cemetery	Wonboyn Beach
Bombala Lookout	Bay Cliff walking track
Nadgee Cape Howe Track	City Rock
Nadgee Beach	Green Cape Lighthouse
Newtons Beach	Quarantine Bay Boat Ramp
Jane Spiers Beach	Quarantine Bay

Eden lookout point

Long Point lookout

Lennards Island

Rotary Park Lookout

Aurora Locations in Sydney, Hoskinstown, Guerilla Bay, Jervis Bay, Beecroft Peninsula, Campbell, Gerroa, Barren Grounds, and Shell Cove

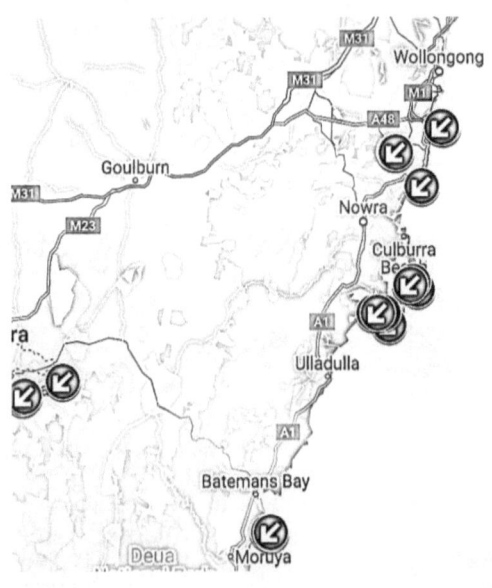

Molonglo Observatory Synthesis Telescope

David Magill Lookout

Guerilla Bay Lookout

Burrewarra Point Lighthouse

Five Mile Beach

Bherwerre Beach

Cave Beach

St George's Head

Point Perpendicular Lighthouse

Dart Point

CHASING AURORA AUSTRALIS

Point Javelin

Silica Cove

Little Target Beach

Gerroa Headland

Illawarra lookout walking track

Barren Grounds Illawarra

Lookout

Bushrangers Bay Aquatic Reserve

Bushrangers Bay Viewing Platform

18
FAQS ON AURORA AUSTRALIS

Here are some frequently asked questions on Southern Lights.

Is it easier to see the northern lights or the southern lights?

It's generally easier to see the Northern Lights (aurora borealis) than the Southern Lights (aurora australis). Here's why:

Population and Accessibility: The Northern Lights are visible from more populated and accessible regions. Countries like Norway, Sweden, Finland, Canada, and Alaska are well-known for aurora viewing, and they offer numerous tours and infrastructure to support aurora hunters. In contrast, the Southern Lights are best seen from remote areas like Antarctica and the southern tips of New Zealand and Tasmania, which are less accessible and have fewer viewing facilities.

Geographical Extent: The Northern Hemisphere has more landmasses extending into high latitudes where auroras are visible. In the Southern Hemisphere, most of the high-latitude regions are covered by the ocean, limiting the number of accessible land-based viewing spots.

Aurora Tourism: Northern regions have developed significant tourism around aurora viewing, with many tour operators, hotels, and guides dedicated to helping visitors experience the Northern Lights. This infrastructure makes it easier for people to plan trips and have successful viewing experiences.

Are the Southern Lights harmful to humans in any way?

The southern lights are just as stunning but appear in harder-to-reach places near the South Pole, such as Antarctica, some parts of mainland Australia, Tasmania, and New Zealand. While amazing, viewing conditions could be better, and catching a glimpse can be more of a gamble than the northern lights.

Is wildlife affected by the Southern Lights?

The Southern Lights don't significantly impact wildlife. Animals might notice the lights, but they aren't harmful. Many nocturnal animals probably carry on with their night as usual, unaware of the stunning display above them. So, while the lights might captivate us, they don't bother the local wildlife.

Do the Southern Lights Make a Sound?

Believe it or not, some people have heard faint sounds during the Southern Lights, like soft crackles or whooshing noises. However, these sounds are rare and need to be scientifically proven. For most of us, the aurora australis is a silent, magical light show. So, while your eyes will be dazzled, your ears probably won't hear a thing!

What are all the shapes of the Aurora?

Picture the night sky as a giant canvas and the Aurora as nature's paintbrush, creating stunning shapes that leave us in awe. The northern and southern lights come in various forms, each more mesmerizing than the last. Let's explore the fantastic shapes of the Aurora and what makes them so unique!

Rippling Curtains

Imagine silky curtains gently fluttering in a breeze, but these curtains glow with vibrant colours! The rippling curtain shape is the most common aurora form. It happens when charged particles from the Sun hit the Earth's magnetic field and follow its lines down to the atmosphere. These particles excite oxygen and nitrogen, creating shimmering green, pink, and sometimes red waves.

Glowing Arcs

Think of a giant rainbow stretching across the night sky, but it's a glowing arc of light instead of a rainbow. These arcs are long, thin bands that span the horizon. They form when the solar wind, a stream of charged particles from the Sun, is steady. The particles glide along the magnetic field lines, creating these graceful arcs.

Pulsating Patches

Imagine the sky sprinkled with glowing patches that appear and disappear like magic. Pulsating patches are spots of light that blink on and off. They can be small and scattered or cover large areas of the sky. These patches form when the solar wind interacts with the Earth's magnetic field in a pulsing rhythm, creating a captivating, blinking effect.

Spirals and Swirls

Now, picture the aurora twisting and turning like someone is stirring a cosmic paint pot. Spirals and swirls occur during times of high solar activity. When the solar wind is strong and turbulent, it twists the Earth's magnetic field lines, creating these swirling shapes. It's like the sky is putting on a dazzling, spinning dance show!

Coronas

Imagine looking straight up at the sky and seeing a burst of light that seems to come from a single point, spreading out in all directions like the rays of the Sun. This shape is called a corona. Coronas happen when you are directly beneath the Aurora's peak. The charged particles dive down along the magnetic field lines and explode into a crown of light right above you.

Rays

Think of giant glowing pencils drawing lines in the sky. These are the aurora rays, which look like straight, bright light beams. Rays form when charged particles flow down narrow channels along the magnetic field lines. They can stand alone or be part of a larger aurora display, adding their sharp, bright lines to the show.

Picket Fence

Imagine a glowing picket fence stretching across the sky. This rare shape looks like vertical bars of light lined up in a row. The picket fence effect occurs when the solar wind moves quickly, causing the charged particles to align in neat, vertical lines.

Will There Be an Aurora Tonight?

No one can say when an aurora will appear in your area, either on camera or by eye. You can check some excellent sources for up-to-date forecasts to find out if there will be an aurora tonight. The NOAA Space Weather Prediction Center has an Aurora Dashboard with northern and southern lights predictions. It features maps and animations showing the expected visibility and intensity for the next 30 minutes and the night ahead.

For a more detailed look, the Geophysical Institute offers predictions based on the Kp index, which measures geomagnetic activity that influences aurora visibility. This can give you a good idea of how active the Aurora might be over the coming nights.

To stay updated with real-time data, download one of the many Aurora forecast apps available.

Where is a Good Spot to see the Southern Lights?

There are many great locations to see the Aurora Australis, but the best views are generally found south of Tasmania and south of New Zealand. When the Aurora is strong, it can also be seen in other parts of Tasmania, New Zealand, and other Australian states.

Are Aurora Forecasts accurate?

Aurora forecasts indicate when and where you might see the Southern Lights, but they are not 100% accurate. Aurora forecasts are based on solar activity, such as flares and coronal mass ejections (CMEs). While we can predict solar activity, it can sometimes be more precise.

Forecasts use the Kp index, a measure of geomagnetic activity, to predict aurora visibility. A higher Kp index means a greater chance of seeing an aurora. However, the exact timing and intensity can vary, as geomagnetic storms can be unpredictable.

Even with accurate solar and geomagnetic data, local conditions such as weather and light pollution play a significant role in whether you can see the Aurora. Clear, dark skies away from city lights are essential for good viewing.

While aurora forecasts are helpful guides, remember to check real-time data and local weather conditions for the best chance of catching the lights.

What will Southern lights look like with the naked eye?

Seeing the Southern Lights with the naked eye can be tricky unless they are incredibly bright. You might notice a faint, coloured glow in the sky where it would usually be pitch black. It's a subtle but magical sight. However, your camera or smartphone can capture way more detail! Longer exposure will reveal vibrant colours and intricate patterns that are hard to see with just your eyes. So, bring a good camera or smartphone to truly capture the beauty of the Southern Lights!

Can You See the Aurora from Space?

The aurora borealis (Northern Lights) and aurora australis (Southern Lights) can be seen from space. Astronauts aboard the International Space Station (ISS) often capture stunning images and videos of these auroras as they fly over the polar regions. From space, auroras appear as significant, glowing rings around the magnetic poles, with vibrant colours and dynamic movements that are truly spectacular.

The view from space provides a unique perspective, showcasing these natural light shows' full scale and beauty. Satellites and space missions regularly observe and study auroras to understand more about their formation and the impact of solar activity on Earth's atmosphere.

Does moonlight affect the Southern Lights?

Moonlight can affect how well you see the Southern Lights, but it doesn't change them. Here's how it works:

When the moon is full or nearly complete, its bright light can wash out the night sky, making it harder to see the auroras. It's similar to how city lights make it difficult to see stars. The Southern Lights are still there, doing their magical dance, but the contrast between the auroras and the sky is less pronounced, making them appear fainter.

On the other hand, when the moon is new, or there's a crescent moon, the sky is much darker, providing a better backdrop for the auroras. This makes the colours and movements of the Southern Lights stand out more vividly.

If you plan to see the Southern Lights, check the moon phase. A darker night will give you a better chance to enjoy this spectacular natural display fully.

How Often Do the Southern Lights Appear?

The Southern Lights don't have a strict schedule, but here's what we know:

Solar Cycle: The frequency of auroras is tied to the solar cycle, which lasts about 11 years. During periods of high solar activity, known as the solar maximum, auroras are more frequent and intense. Conversely, during the solar minimum, they are less common.

Seasonal Peaks: Auroras are more likely to occur during the equinoxes in March and September. These times of year have the best conditions for geomagnetic activity, increasing the chances of seeing the Southern Lights.

Location Matters: The further south you go, the better your chances. Places like Antarctica, Tasmania, and the southern parts of New Zealand are prime spots. However, clear, dark skies free from light pollution are essential even in these locations.

Unpredictable Nature: Auroras are influenced by solar storms and geomagnetic activity, making them unpredictable.

Keeping an eye on aurora forecasts and space weather updates can help you catch these stunning displays when they occur.

While the Southern Lights may not appear every night, with the right conditions and a bit of luck, you can experience this mesmerizing phenomenon.

How Long Does an Aurora Last?

Auroras can put on quite a show, and their duration can vary greatly, adding to the excitement! Here's what to expect:

Quick Flashes: Sometimes, auroras appear as brief bursts of light that last only a few minutes. These quick displays are like nature's teasing us with a spectacular yet fleeting light show.

Extended Performances: Other times, auroras can linger for several hours, fluctuating in intensity and colour. These more extended displays can transform the sky into a dynamic and mesmerizing canvas that is constantly changing and captivating.

Geomagnetic Activity: The length and intensity of an aurora depend on geomagnetic activity. Strong solar storms can create prolonged and intense auroras, while weaker activity might result in shorter, less vivid displays. So, the more active the geomagnetic conditions, the longer the show!

Nightly Variations: During a single night, auroras can come and go, with periods of increased activity followed by quieter times. This means you might witness multiple aurora bursts throughout the night, varying in duration and intensity.

Auroras can last a few minutes to several hours, depending on solar and geomagnetic activity. Watch space weather forecasts and be ready for a night of changing conditions and stunning views!

Do sunspots affect the Southern Lights?

Yes, sunspots can affect the Southern Lights! Here's how it works:

Sunspots are dark spots on the Sun's surface that are cooler than the surrounding areas. They are associated with increased solar activity, including solar flares and coronal mass ejections (CMEs). These events release a large amount of charged particles into space.

When these charged particles reach Earth, they interact with our planet's magnetic field and atmosphere, causing the auroras. The more intense the solar activity, the more spectacular the auroras can be. So, during periods of high sunspot activity, you are more likely to see more robust and more frequent displays of the Southern Lights.

Is the Sun heading towards a new Maunder Minimum?

The idea that the Sun might be heading towards a new Maunder Minimum has been a scientific discussion and speculation topic. The Maunder Minimum was deficient in solar activity between approximately 1645 and 1715. Significantly few sunspots were observed during this time, coinciding with the "Little Ice Age," a period of cooler global temperatures.

The recent solar cycles have shown a trend toward lower activity than the peak activity in the mid-20th century. For example, Solar Cycle 24, which peaked around 2014, was notably weaker than previous cycles. Solar Cycle 25, which began in December 2019, is expected to be similar in activity to Solar Cycle 24.

While some evidence suggests that we might be heading towards a period of lower solar activity, it is still uncertain whether it will be as pronounced as the Maunder Minimum. Ongoing observations and research are essential to improving our understanding of solar cycles and their potential impacts on Earth.

Will the Aurora Completely Disappear During Solar Minimum?

Nope! The Aurora doesn't vanish during solar minimum; it just becomes less frequent. There's still a chance to see the lights, especially if you're in a prime location, so keep an eye on the forecasts. So, don't give up hope—those magical displays can still surprise you!

I Want to Buy a Camera for Aurora Photography. What Should I Consider?

Here's what you need for capturing those stunning auroras:

Camera: Get a DSLR or mirrorless camera with manual settings. These allow you to adjust exposure, ISO, and focus, which is crucial for night photography.

Lens: Look for a wide-angle lens with a large aperture (like f/2.8 or lower f-stop). This helps capture as much light as possible, making those auroras pop.

Tripod: Remember a sturdy tripod. Long exposure shots require a steady camera, and a tripod will keep everything stable and sharp.

What's the difference between Kp5 and G1?

Kp5 and G1 are like two sides of the same coin. Kp5 measures geomagnetic activity, while G1 is a classification for a minor geomagnetic storm. When the Kp index hits 5, we're in G1 territory, which means a minor storm and a good chance for auroras!

What are Long-Duration and Impulsive Solar Flares?

Think of solar flares as fireworks from the Sun. Long-duration flares are like those grand finale fireworks that light up the sky for a while—they last for hours and often lead to enormous coronal mass ejections (CMEs). Impulsive flares, on the other hand, are like quick, bright bursts—they happen fast, in just minutes, and are over before you know it. Both are spectacular but in their unique way!

Why is Antarctica Perfect for Aurora Viewing?

Location, Location, Location: Antarctica is under the aurora oval, a ring-shaped zone around the magnetic poles where auroras are most likely to occur. This makes it one of the best places on Earth to see the aurora australis.

Dark Skies: With little to no light pollution, Antarctica offers some of the darkest skies on the planet. This means the auroras can appear brighter and more intense, providing an unforgettable viewing experience.

Long Nights: During the Antarctic winter (from March to September), the continent experiences extended periods of darkness, sometimes even 24-hour nights. This gives you plenty of opportunities to catch the Aurora in action.

What is an Earth-Directed Aurora?

An Earth-directed aurora happens when a burst of solar energy from the Sun is aimed directly at Earth. This energy interacts with our planet's magnetic field, creating bright and intense auroras that can light up the sky in ways that feel almost personal like the universe is putting on a special show just for us.

The Sun constantly sends out charged particles, known as the solar wind. Sometimes, the Sun gets particularly active and releases a powerful burst of energy called a coronal mass ejection (CME). When this CME is aimed directly at Earth, it's like the Sun throws a cosmic fastball at us.

When charged particles from the Sun hit Earth's magnetic field, they are funnelled towards the poles. The magnetic field lines guide the particles into the upper atmosphere, colliding with gases like oxygen and nitrogen. These collisions release energy in the form of light, creating the beautiful auroras we see.

Earth-directed auroras are often more intense and widespread than usual auroras. Because the energy is aimed directly at us, the resulting light show can be incredibly bright and colourful, with vivid greens, reds, blues, and purples dancing across the sky. Sometimes, these auroras can even be seen farther away from the poles than usual, giving more people a chance to witness the spectacle.

One of the exciting aspects of Earth-Directed Auroras is the anticipation. Scientists use satellites and solar observatories to monitor the Sun's activity and predict when a CME is headed our way. This means you can get a heads-up to prepare for an aurora sighting, making the experience even more thrilling.

While most auroras are best seen near the polar regions, Earth-Directed Auroras can sometimes be visible much farther south or north than usual. This means people in places that don't typically see auroras might get a rare and beautiful treat. It's like a global invitation to join in the cosmic celebration.

Although Earth-Directed Auroras are beautiful, the energy from a CME can also affect our technology. It can disrupt satellites, communication systems, and even power grids. Scientists work hard to predict these events so we can protect our technology while still enjoying the incredible light show.

What would happen if the Carrington event were to happen today?

In 1859, British astronomer Richard Carrington observed a massive solar flare, followed by a substantial coronal mass ejection (CME) aimed directly at Earth. Within hours, the solar particles slammed into our planet's magnetic field, causing spectacular auroras visible as far south as the Caribbean and north as Queensland. If these were to happen today, this is what we can expect:

Spectacular Auroras: First off, we'd be treated to breathtaking auroras far beyond the polar regions. People in places like Florida and Spain could see the night sky lit up with vibrant greens, reds, and purples. It would be like a global light show!

Power Grid Problems: The geomagnetic storm could induce powerful electric currents in power lines, potentially overloading and damaging transformers. This could lead to widespread power outages, possibly lasting days or weeks in some areas.

Satellite Disruption: Our satellites, which control everything from GPS navigation to communication networks, would be at risk. The intense radiation could disrupt signals and even damage the satellites themselves. Imagine using your GPS or making a phone call and finding nothing works!

Communication Blackouts: High-frequency radio communications used by airplanes and ships could be knocked out. This could create navigation challenges and require a return to more traditional methods of communication and navigation.

Internet Outages: Undersea cables that connect global internet infrastructure could be affected, leading to slowdowns or outages. The internet as we know it could experience significant disruptions, affecting businesses, entertainment, and even daily life.

Radiation Exposure: The International Space Station (ISS) astronauts must shelter in specially protected areas to avoid harmful radiation. Even passengers on high-altitude flights could be exposed to increased levels of radiation.

How can protons from eruptions on the far side possibly reach Earth sometimes?

Imagine the Sun as a vast cosmic smoothie blender. When it blends up a storm on the far side, the energetic protons can still find their way around to us. These sneaky protons travel along the Sun's magnetic field lines, which twist and turn through space, allowing them to reach Earth even if the flare happens on the Sun's far side.

I read about a Solar Flare Today. Will We See the Aurora Tonight?

Not quite! A solar flare by itself doesn't cause auroras. Solar flares can launch vast clouds of solar plasma, known as coronal mass ejections (CMEs). It's these CMEs that can trigger auroras when they hit Earth. But here's the catch—not every solar flare sends out a CME. Most don't!

Even if we get a big, eruptive solar flare, it needs to come from a sunspot near the centre of the Earth-facing side of the Sun. Otherwise, the CME might miss Earth entirely. While the light from a solar flare reaches us in just 8 minutes, CMEs travel much slower. The fastest CMEs can make the trip in about a day, but usually, they take two to four days to arrive.

What Kp-Values are needed to see the Aurora at my location?

Australia

Tasmania (Hobart)

Kp 4-5: There is a moderate chance of seeing the Aurora, especially in southern parts of Tasmania.
Kp 6-7: Good visibility across most of Tasmania, including Hobart.
Kp 8+: Excellent visibility across all of Tasmania.

Victoria (Melbourne)

Kp 7-8: It is possible to see the Aurora, especially from dark, rural areas away from city lights.

Kp 9+: High likelihood of visibility, particularly in southern parts of the state.

New South Wales (Sydney)

Kp 8-9: Infrequent but possible during intense geomagnetic storms. It is best viewed from dark, elevated locations.

South Australia (Adelaide)

Kp 7-8: Possible visibility, especially in rural areas away from light pollution.

Kp 9+: Likely to see the Aurora, especially in southern parts of the state.

Australian Capital Territory (Canberra)

Kp 8-9: Infrequent but possible during intense geomagnetic storms. It is best viewed from dark, elevated locations away from city lights.

Western Australia (Perth)

Kp 8-9: Rare, but during powerful geomagnetic storms, there might be a slight chance to see the Aurora from dark locations in the southern parts of the state.

New Zealand

South Island (Stewart Island, Dunedin)

Kp 4-5: There is a moderate chance of seeing the Aurora, particularly from dark, southern locations like Stewart Island.

Kp 6-7: Good visibility across much of the South Island, including Dunedin.

Kp 8+: Excellent visibility across the entire South Island.

North Island (Wellington)

Kp 7-8: It is possible to see the Aurora from southern parts of the North Island, including Wellington.

Kp 9+: Likely to see the Aurora, especially from dark locations.

What is a white-light solar flare?

White-light solar flares are like the VIPs of solar events. Most flares emit X-rays and UV light, but white-light flares are so powerful that they're visible in regular white light, too! It's like seeing a super bright flash of lightning during the day—rare and imposing.

I hear people talking about Eastern Limb and Western Limb of the Sun. Can you explain?

The Sun constantly rotates, taking about 27 days to complete one full turn. This rotation affects where we see solar activity:

Eastern Limb: The edge of the Sun that rotates into view

from our perspective on Earth. When solar activity like sunspots, flares, or CMEs are observed on the eastern limb, they become visible and may affect Earth as they rotate into direct view.

Western Limb: The edge of the Sun rotating out of view. Solar activity on the western limb moves away from Earth's direct line of sight. While these features may still impact space weather, they are less likely to affect auroras than activity on the eastern limb directly.

What are the Solar Features and Their Impact on Auroras?

The Sun, our dynamic and fiery star, plays a crucial role in creating the breathtaking auroras we see on Earth. To understand how different parts of the Sun contribute to these magical light shows, let's take a tour of the Sun and its features.

First, let's get familiar with the main parts of the Sun:

Core: The Sun's core is its powerhouse, where nuclear fusion occurs, producing enormous amounts of energy.

Radiative Zone: Surrounding the core, this layer transports energy outward through radiation.

Convective Zone: Energy moves through convection currents, bringing heat to the surface.

Photosphere: This is the visible surface of the Sun that we see from Earth. It's where sunspots and solar flares can occur.

Chromosphere: A layer above the photosphere, visible during solar eclipses, appearing as a reddish glow.

Corona: The outermost layer of the Sun's atmosphere, extending millions of kilometres into space, visible during a total solar eclipse.

Now, let's dive into the specific features and how they relate to auroras:

Sunspots are dark spots on the photosphere caused by intense magnetic activity. Sunspots are often the birthplace of solar flares and coronal mass ejections (CMEs), which can trigger auroras when their charged particles reach Earth.

Solar Flares: Sudden, intense bursts of radiation from the Sun's surface near sunspots. When directed toward Earth, these flares can release a flood of charged particles into space, enhancing auroras.

Coronal Mass Ejections (CMEs): Massive bursts of solar wind and magnetic fields rising above the solar corona or being released into space. When these CMEs are directed towards Earth, they interact with our magnetic field, causing spectacular auroras.

How to Dress for Aurora Hunting?

Aurora hunting is an exciting adventure; dressing right is essential for warmth and comfort. Think of yourself as an onion, layering up to trap heat and block the cold.

Start with a moisture-wicking base layer.
Add a warm insulating layer.
Finish with a waterproof and windproof outer layer.
Head: Wear a warm hat or balaclava to cover your ears and protect your face.
Hands: Choose insulated, waterproof gloves or mittens.
Feet: Wear thick wool socks and waterproof, insulated boots with good traction.

To enhance your experience, bring hand warmers, a cozy

blanket or sleeping bag, and a thermal mat. Also, remember to use a thermos of hot beverages, high-energy snacks, and a red light setting for better visibility in the dark.

Why is it difficult to accurately determine the magnetic arrangement of sunspot regions near the edges of the Sun?

Think of the Sun as a giant ball. When you look at the edges (the limbs), you see things at an angle, distorting the view. It's like trying to read a book sideways—you can see the words, but it's hard to make out the details. Sunspots near the limbs appear squished and tilted, making it tricky to map their magnetic fields accurately.

Do sunspot regions observed by STEREO on the far side of the Sun receive an identification number?

No! Sunspot regions spotted by STEREO on the far side get official numbers once they rotate to the Earth-facing side. It's like a player waiting on the bench—they're not in the game until they're on the field, where we can see them directly from Earth.

Do Coronal Holes reappear after 27 days?

Coronal holes are areas on the Sun's surface where the magnetic field lines open up, allowing solar wind to escape into space. These holes appear dark in images because they are more relaxed and less dense than the surrounding areas. Think of them as open windows letting the solar wind flow into the solar system.

The Sun takes about 27 days to complete one full rotation on its axis. If you could mark a spot on the Sun and wait 27 days, that spot would return to face you again. This rotation period is why coronal holes reappear every 27 days.

If a coronal hole is stable and doesn't change much over time, it will rotate with the Sun and come back into view roughly every 27 days.

Stable Coronal Holes: These are like the Sun's signature dance moves. If a coronal hole is stable, it can persist for several rotations, reappearing every 27 days.

Changing Coronal Holes: Sometimes, the Sun's magnetic field changes, causing coronal holes to evolve or disappear. If a coronal hole changes significantly, it might not reappear precisely the same way.

Knowing that coronal holes can reappear every 27 days helps scientists predict space weather. The high-speed solar wind flowing from these holes can cause geomagnetic storms on Earth, leading to stunning auroras and sometimes disrupting satellites and communication systems.

What's the difference between IMF North and IMF South?

The IMF can point in different directions, just like you can face north, south, east, or west. When discussing "% -ve in IMF," we focus on how much it points south.

This is important because:

Northward IMF (Positive): When the IMF points north, it aligns with Earth's magnetic field. Imagine two dancers moving in the same direction—they glide smoothly without much fuss. This usually means fewer disturbances and weaker auroras.

Southward IMF (Negative): When the IMF points south, it opposes Earth's magnetic field. Now, imagine the dancers facing opposite directions and bumping into each other. This causes a magnetic reconnection, releasing energy and allowing charged particles to pour into Earth's atmosphere, creating brighter and more intense auroras.

What causes diffuse Aurora?

Diffuse auroras are caused by a steady, less intense solar wind flow. Imagine the solar wind as a calm breeze rather than a strong gust. When this gentle flow of particles reaches Earth, it doesn't create dramatic, colourful curtains of light. Instead, it spreads out more evenly across the sky, creating a soft, diffuse glow.

Are Auroras Predictable?

Auroras are like the universe's spontaneous dance parties! While they have a mind of their own, we can make some good guesses about when they might show up.

Scientists use space weather forecasts to predict auroras. When the Sun sends a burst of charged particles toward Earth, known as a solar storm, these particles interact with our atmosphere and create the beautiful lights we see. Experts can often tell when an aurora is likely to occur by watching the Sun and measuring these particles.

However, it's not an exact science. It's like predicting a surprise party—you get some clues, but the exact time and place can still catch you off guard. Websites and apps can help you keep track of aurora forecasts, so you'll have a heads-up when there's a good chance of seeing these fantastic lights.

What's a Substorm?

A substorm is like a sudden burst of excitement in the sky's light show! Imagine you're at a concert, and when you think the music can't get any better, the band kicks it up a notch. That's what happens during a substorm with auroras.

More scientifically, a substorm is a temporary disturbance in the Earth's magnetosphere. When the Sun sends charged particles toward Earth, they interact with our planet's magnetic field. Sometimes, this interaction builds up suddenly released energy, causing the auroras to brighten and dance more wildly than usual.

During a substorm, the auroras can go from a calm, gentle glow to a vibrant, swirling spectacle in minutes. The lights can spread across the sky, creating waves, curtains, and even spirals of colour.

What's a Magnetometer?

A magnetometer is like a super cool gadget that spies on the Earth's magnetic field! Think of it as a magical compass with superpowers. While a regular compass points you north, a magnetometer measures the strength and direction of magnetic fields around it.

Scientists and aurora hunters use magnetometers to monitor the Earth's magnetic field. When the Sun sends charged particles our way, they can cause changes in the magnetic field, and that's where the magnetometer comes in. It can detect these changes and help predict when auroras might light up the sky.

What are Geomagnetic Substorm and explain Growth/Expansion/Recovery Phases?

A geomagnetic substorm is like a surprise fireworks show in space! An intense burst of activity in the Earth's magnetosphere causes auroras to light up spectacularly.

Let's break down the three phases of this cosmic event:

Growth Phase

Picture this: it's like the warm-up act before the main concert. During the growth phase, the Sun's charged particles build energy in the Earth's magnetic field. The auroras might glow softly, like the stage lights dimming before the big performance. This phase can last for about 30 to 60 minutes.

Expansion Phase

Now, the real show begins! The expansion phase is when things get exciting. The built-up energy is suddenly released, causing the auroras to burst into bright, dancing lights. The sky can go from a gentle glow to a vibrant, swirling spectacle. This phase is like the crescendo of a symphony, where everything is at its peak. It usually lasts 10 to 30 minutes, but it's the most thrilling part of the substorm.

Recovery Phase

After the grand finale, the lights start to calm down. The recovery phase is like the gentle encore after the main event. The auroras gradually fade to a softer glow as the magnetic field settles. This phase can take several hours, giving you a lingering sense of the magical show you've just witnessed.

Why a Kp or K Index that is not accurate for predicting Southern Lights?

The Kp or K Index is like the Aurora weather forecast! On a scale from 0 to 9, it tells us how active the Earth's magnetic field is. A higher Kp index means more geomagnetic activity, which usually means a better chance of seeing auroras.

But here's the catch: the Kp index could better predict the Southern Lights. It's mainly based on data from the Northern Hemisphere, so it sometimes gives a better picture of what's happening down south. Think of it as using weather reports from one city to predict the weather in another – sometimes it works, but it's not always spot on.

The Southern Lights, or Aurora Australis, are influenced by different factors and can behave differently from the Northern Lights. Local conditions, like weather and magnetic field variations, also play a significant role. So, while the Kp index can give you a hint, there are more reliable tools for Southern Lights. It's good to check local Aurora forecasts and watch real-time updates for the best chances of catching the Southern Lights.

The Kaus Index is your go-to superhero for measuring geomagnetic activity Down Under! It's like having a weather forecast for the sky, updating every five minutes to give you near real-time readings of the K index for Australia.

What are G1, G2 and G3?

G1, G2, and G3 are like the weather grades for geomagnetic storms, telling us how intense these space weather events are.

G1 – Minor Storm

A G1 storm is like a light sprinkle of excitement. It's a minor geomagnetic storm that might cause some beautiful auroras visible at higher latitudes. It's like a gentle warm-up, with some flickering lights in the sky. These storms can cause minor impacts on power grids and satellite operations, but nothing too dramatic.

G2 – Moderate Storm

Now, we're getting into the good stuff! A G2 storm is a moderate geomagnetic storm. This one cranks up the intensity, and the auroras can be seen further away from the poles. Imagine the sky lighting up with more vibrant colours and more dynamic movements. It's like a great night at the movies with some thrilling scenes!

G3 – Strong Storm

A G3 storm is when things get seriously exciting. It's a solid geomagnetic storm that can create stunning auroras visible much further from the poles, sometimes even in regions where you wouldn't usually see them. Think of it as the blockbuster hit of the geomagnetic world, with dazzling lights filling the sky. These storms can cause disruptions to power systems and satellite operations, making it a space-weather adventure!

What's Hemispheric Power?

Hemispheric Power is like the energy meter for the auroras! It measures how much power, in gigawatts, is being dumped into the Earth's atmosphere by the solar wind, creating those fantastic light shows we call auroras.

Think of it as the brightness dial on nature's light show. The higher the hemispheric power, the more intense and widespread the auroras are likely. It's like turning up the volume at a concert—the higher the dial goes, the more spectacular the performance.

When scientists talk about hemispheric power, they look at how much energy is being delivered to the Northern and Southern Hemispheres. If the hemispheric power is high, you can expect more robust and vibrant auroras, possibly visible at lower latitudes.

Do returning sunspot regions receive a new number when reappearing on the Earth-facing solar disk?

Yes, they do! When sunspot regions return to the Earth-facing side of the Sun, they get a brand-new number. They've returned from a vacation with a fresh new identity, ready to be tracked and studied again.

What's a CH HSS?

A CH HSS, or Coronal Hole High-Speed Stream, is like the Sun blowing us a high-speed kiss! Imagine the Sun with areas on its surface called coronal holes, where the magnetic field opens up and lets out solar wind streams. These streams are like gusts of charged particles that zoom through space at super-fast speeds.

When a CH HSS heads towards Earth, it can interact with our planet's magnetic field, stirring things up and creating beautiful auroras. It's like the Sun sending a fast and furious wave of energy our way, adding some extra sparkle to the night sky.

CH HSS events aren't as dramatic as CMEs, but they happen more frequently and can still cause minor geomagnetic storms.

What are the Pitfalls of the Kp index?

The Kp index is like a general aurora weather forecast but has quirks and pitfalls. Here's why it's not always perfect for predicting auroras, especially the Southern Lights:

Northern Bias

The Kp index is mainly based on data from the Northern Hemisphere. It's like trying to predict the weather in Australia using forecasts from Canada. Sometimes, it works, but often, it needs to do better for the Southern Hemisphere.

Broad Brush

The Kp index gives a global picture of geomagnetic activity, but it's like saying, "It's going to be hot somewhere on Earth today." It doesn't give detailed info about specific locations, so that you might miss out on local aurora chances.

Time Lag

The Kp index updates every three hours, which is great, but space weather can change quickly. It's like checking yesterday's weather report to plan your beach day today. You may miss out on real-time changes that affect Aurora's visibility.

Not a Perfect Predictor

Auroras are influenced by many factors, not just the Kp index. Local weather, geographic location, and even magnetic field disturbances play a role. Relying solely on the Kp index is like using a single ingredient to bake a cake—it's essential, but it's not the whole recipe.

Southern Lights Overlooked

Because the Kp index is designed with the Northern Hemisphere in mind, it often doesn't capture the nuances needed to predict the Southern Lights accurately. It's like using a northern map to navigate southern waters—helpful but not precise.

So, while the Kp index is a helpful tool, it's best to use it alongside other resources and local forecasts.

Why can't we see the southern lights with the naked eye as clearly as they appear in photographs?

Cameras are like tech-savvy friends who consistently get the best concert photos, even from the nosebleed seats. They can capture more light than our human eyes can. They hold the shutter open longer, soaking in every photon like a sponge, making those auroras pop with colour.

Our eyes, on the other hand, are more like that friend who insists on using a flip phone in 2024. They're great for everyday stuff, but they struggle to keep up in low light.

The southern lights, or aurora australis if you feel fancy, are often subtle and delicate. The colours can be faint and blend into the night sky. With their superpowers, cameras pick up on these faint lights and enhance them, making them look like a cosmic rave party. Our eyes, unfortunately, are more like the partygoers who showed up too early—the lights are there, but they're not quite in full swing yet.

So next time you're out there, squinting at the sky, remember: your eyes are doing their best. They're just not equipped with the same magical powers as a camera. You've got hot chocolate, a cozy blanket, and the great outdoors. Sometimes, that's more than enough.

There is an Aurora forecast for the whole weekend. Does it mean there will be Aurora all weekend?

So, you've heard there's an aurora forecast for the whole weekend, and you're thinking, "Sweet! A non-stop cosmic light show!" Let's pump the brakes just a tad and dive into the delightful unpredictability of nature's sky-high pyrotechnics.

An Aurora forecast is kind of like your quirky friend who promises an epic weekend party. They say it's happening all weekend, but you know there's a chance they'll get sidetracked by a new hobby, like extreme knitting or competitive napping. The forecast suggests that conditions are ripe for the aurora to appear, but it doesn't guarantee that the lights will be dancing overhead non-stop.

Think of it like the weather forecast: just because it says it might rain all weekend doesn't mean there will be a constant downpour. There will be breaks, maybe some sunshine, and definitely moments when you're questioning the accuracy of that app you rely on. Auroras are the same—they can be fickle and elusive, showing up in bursts and waves rather than putting on a steady show.

Here's the fun part: the forecast means there's a good chance you'll catch the aurora at some point. It's like having multiple raffle tickets for a prize drawing. The more tickets you have, the better your odds, but there's still a bit of luck involved. So, grab your warm gear, camera (to capture those sneaky, faint lights), and maybe a cozy blanket. Get ready for a weekend of sky-watching where patience and a bit of luck are your best buddies.

What's a common rookie mistake when it comes to chasing Aurora?

Let's set the scene: you're all pumped for a night of aurora hunting. You've got your gear ready, your cozy clothes on, and your camera primed. But then, you think, "Hey, why not have a nice, leisurely dinner first? The aurora will wait, right?" One of the most common rookie mistakes.

Auroras are like that elusive pop-up food truck with the best tacos in town. They show up unannounced, hang around for a bit, and then poof—they're gone, leaving only whispers and Instagram posts behind. Deciding to head out after dinner could mean missing the main event entirely.

You finish your meal, maybe linger over dessert, and finally head out, only to find out that while you savour that last bite, the aurora puts on a spectacular show and vanishes. Timing is everything with auroras. They don't run on your schedule;

you've got to be ready to drop everything and head out when the conditions are right. The urgency of the moment, the need to be prepared and quick, adds a thrilling element to the aurora chase.

So, here's the tip: when the forecast says there's a good chance for an aurora, treat it like a flash sale on your favourite gear. Get out early, bring a snack, and don't assume you can catch it later. Be ready, be quick, and let dinner be what you do while you wait for the lights, not the other way around.

19
SPACE WEATHER GLOSSARY

Acronyms and abbreviations can often feel like a foreign language in space weather reports, leaving many feeling excluded. But fear not – we're here to bridge that gap! In this chapter, you'll find a user-friendly list of the most commonly used terms, each explained in a way that's easy to understand. We want everyone, from enthusiasts to researchers and students, to feel welcomed and included in the world of space weather. So, let's start decoding together!

1. ADF (Active Dark Filament)

An Active Dark Filament (ADF) is a long, dark ribbon of cooler gas suspended above the Sun's surface. It's like a twisted rope of solar material hanging out and waiting to cause some space-weather drama.

2. AIA (Atmospheric Imaging Assembly)

The Atmospheric Imaging Assembly is a Solar Dynamics Observatory (SDO) camera set. It's like a high-tech paparazzi crew capturing stunning images of the Sun in different wavelengths.

3. AR (Active Region)

An Active Region on the Sun has strong magnetic fields that can produce solar flares and CMEs. Think of it as a hotspot where all the solar action happens!

4. APR (Active Prominence Region)

An Active Prominence Region is an area on the Sun where huge, bright loops of gas erupt. It's like a fiery fountain of solar plasma putting on a spectacular show. To put it in perspective, imagine a volcano on Earth, but instead of lava, it's spewing out solar plasma!

5. ASR (Active Surge Region)

An Active Surge Region is a part of the Sun where energetic eruptions of material occur. It's like a geyser on the Sun, shooting out plasma in powerful bursts. To break it down, 'active' means 'energetic and eruptive ', 'surge' refers to a sudden increase or burst, and 'region' is a specific area on the Sun's surface.

6. BBSO (Big Bear Solar Observatory)

The Big Bear Solar Observatory is a research facility in California dedicated to studying the Sun. It's like a solar laboratory where scientists closely watch our star.

7. BSD (Bright Surge on the Disk)

A Bright Surge on the Disk is a sudden, bright jet of material shooting up from the Sun's surface. It's like a solar flare but more localized and impressive.

8. BSL (Bright Surge on the Limb)

A Bright Surge on the Limb is a bright jet of solar material seen at the edge of the Sun. It's like seeing a solar splash from the side, creating a dazzling edge-on display.

9. CH (Coronal Hole)

A Coronal Hole is a dark area on the Sun's surface where the magnetic field is open, allowing solar wind to escape. It's like a windy gap in the Sun's atmosphere, sending out streams of particles.

10. CIR (Corotating Interaction Region)

Corotating Interaction Regions are areas in the solar wind where fast and slow streams collide. It's like a space traffic jam that can lead to geomagnetic storms when it reaches Earth.

11. CME (Coronal Mass Ejection)

A Coronal Mass Ejection is like the Sun sneezing out a giant bubble of plasma and magnetic field. These solar burps can cause stunning auroras and mess with Earth's magnetic field.

12. CMP (Central Meridian Passage)

Central Meridian Passage is when a solar feature, like a sunspot, crosses the imaginary line down the Sun's centre. It's like a cosmic parade crossing the Sun's central avenue.

13. CRN (Coronal Rain)

Coronal Rain is when cooled plasma falls back to the Sun's

surface from the corona. It's like a gentle solar drizzle, but instead of water, it's raining plasma!

14. CTM (Continuum Storm)

A Continuum Storm is a prolonged period of increased radio noise from the Sun. It's like the Sun turning up the volume on its radio broadcasts, creating static in space.

15. DSD (Dark Surge on the Disk)

A Dark Surge on the Disk is a sudden, dark jet of material shooting up from the Sun's surface. It's like a shadowy splash of solar plasma, adding some dramatic flair.

16. DSF (Disappearing Solar Filament)

A Disappearing Solar Filament is a long, dark ribbon of solar material that suddenly vanishes, often triggering a CME. It's like the Sun pulling a disappearing act with a flourish.

17. DSCOVR (Deep Space Climate Observatory)

The Deep Space Climate Observatory monitors space weather from a special spot between Earth and the Sun. It's like a cosmic weatherman, providing real-time data on solar wind and magnetic storms.

18. Dst (Disturbance Storm Time)

The Disturbance Storm Time index measures the intensity of geomagnetic storms. It's like the Earth's magnetic field getting a strength test during space weather events.

19. EIT (Extreme Ultraviolet Imaging Telescope)

The Extreme Ultraviolet Imaging Telescope takes

incredible pictures of the Sun in ultraviolet light. It's like having UV sunglasses that let us see the Sun's hot outer layers.

20. EPAM (Electron, Proton, and Alpha Monitor)

The Electron, Proton, and Alpha Monitors track charged particles in space. They are like space weather scouts, warning us about incoming particle storms.

21. ESD (Electrostatic Discharge)

Electrostatic Discharge is a sudden flow of electricity between two charged objects. It's like a mini lightning bolt, often caused by space weather affecting satellites.

22. ESA (European Space Agency)

The European Space Agency is Europe's gateway to space. It launches satellites, explores planets, and monitors space weather, like Europe's own space superheroes.

23. EUV (Extreme Ultraviolet)

Extreme Ultraviolet light is a type of light from the Sun that is invisible to our eyes but useful for studying solar activity. It's like the Sun's secret ultraviolet language.

24. EVE (Extreme Ultraviolet Variability Experiment)

The Extreme Ultraviolet Variability Experiment measures how the Sun's ultraviolet light changes over time. It's like tracking the Sun's UV mood swings.

25. GFZ (German Research Centre for Geosciences)

The German Research Centre for Geosciences studies everything from earthquakes to space weather. They're like the scientific detectives of Earth and space.

26. GIC (Geomagnetically Induced Current)

Geomagnetically Induced Currents are electric currents that flow in the Earth's surface during geomagnetic storms. They're like Earth's electric veins getting a power surge.

27. GOES (Geostationary Operational Environmental Satellite)

GOES satellites monitor Earth's weather and space from a fixed spot above the planet. They're like the vigilant guardians of our skies.

28. HMI (Helioseismic and Magnetic Imager)

The Helioseismic and Magnetic Imager study the Sun's magnetic field and internal movements. It is like an ultrasound machine for the Sun, revealing its inner secrets.

29. HPI (Hemispherical Power Input)

Hemispherical Power Input measures the energy input from the solar wind into Earth's atmosphere in each hemisphere. It's like checking how much solar juice each half of the planet gets.

30. HSC (Heliospheric Science Center)

The Heliospheric Science Center studies the space environment influenced by the Sun. It's like the headquarters for understanding how the Sun affects the solar system.

31. HSS (High-Speed Stream)

High-Speed Streams are fast solar winds from coronal

holes. They zoom through space like gusts of wind, causing geomagnetic storms when they reach Earth.

32. IMF (Interplanetary Magnetic Field)

The Interplanetary Magnetic Field is the magnetic field carried by the solar wind. It's like the Sun's magnetic arms reaching out into space, which plays a significant role in space weather.

33. IRIS (Interface Region Imaging Spectrograph)

The Interface Region Imaging Spectrograph studies the Sun's lower atmosphere. It's like a magnifying glass, zooming in on the Sun's dynamic and fiery interface region.

34. L1 (Lagrange Point 1)

L1 is a unique point between Earth and the Sun where gravitational forces balance out. It's the perfect location for satellites to monitor space weather.

35. LASCO (Large Angle and Spectrometric Coronagraph)

The Large Angle and Spectrometric Coronagraph is a camera on the SOHO spacecraft that blocks the Sun's bright light to see the corona. It's like wearing sunglasses to see the Sun's halo.

36. LMSAL (Lockheed Martin Solar and Astrophysics Laboratory)

The Lockheed Martin Solar and Astrophysics Laboratory is a research centre studying the Sun and space weather.

37. MDI (Michelson Doppler Imager)

The Michelson Doppler Imager was an instrument on the SOHO spacecraft that studied solar oscillations and magnetic fields. It's like a Doppler radar for the Sun, showing how it moves and shakes.

38. MLSO (Mauna Loa Solar Observatory)

The Mauna Loa Solar Observatory in Hawaii observes the Sun daily and captures its every move. It's like a sunny vacation spot for solar scientists.

39. NASA (National Aeronautics and Space Administration)

NASA is the US government agency responsible for space exploration, research, and monitoring space weather. They're the pioneers of the final frontier, sending rockets and satellites into the cosmos.

40. NOAA (National Oceanic and Atmospheric Administration)

NOAA monitors oceans, weather, and space weather. It is the guardian of Earth's environment below and above the atmosphere.

41. nT (nanotesla)

A nanotesla is a unit of measurement for magnetic fields. It's like the ruler for measuring the strength of Earth's magnetic field during space weather events.

42. PFU (Proton Flux Unit)

The Proton Flux Unit measures the number of protons passing through a square centimetre every second. It's like counting protons in a cosmic rainstorm.

43. PlasMag (Plasma and Magnetometer Instrument)

The Plasma and Magnetometer Instrument measures plasma and magnetic fields in space. It's like a space weather toolkit, helping us understand the cosmic environment.

44. PROBA2 (Project for On-Board Autonomy 2)

PROBA2 is a small ESA satellite that studies the Sun and space weather.

45. SAA (South Atlantic Anomaly)

The South Atlantic Anomaly is a region where Earth's inner radiation belt comes closest to the surface. In space, it behaves like a Bermuda Triangle, causing issues for satellites and spacecraft.

46. SC (Sudden Commencement)

Sudden Commencement refers to the abrupt start of a geomagnetic storm. It's like the opening act of a space weather concert, signalling that a storm is about to hit Earth's magnetic field.

47. SDO (Solar Dynamics Observatory)

The Solar Dynamics Observatory watches the Sun 24/7, capturing detailed images and data.

48. SIDC (Solar Influences Data Analysis Center)

The Solar Influences Data Analysis Center is a Belgian centre that monitors solar activity and space weather. They're like the space weather analysts, keeping tabs on the Sun's every move.

49. SI (Sudden Impulse)

A Sudden Impulse is a quick jump in Earth's magnetic field strength, usually from a solar wind shockwave. It's like a jolt of energy hitting our planet's magnetic shield.

50. SIR (Stream Interaction Region)

Stream Interaction Regions are areas where fast and slow solar winds collide, creating space weather effects. It's like a solar wind traffic jam causing cosmic disturbances.

51. SOHO (Solar and Heliospheric Observatory)

The Solar and Heliospheric Observatory is a spacecraft that observes the outer layer of the Sun and its solar wind. It functions like a space weather station, providing daily reports on solar activity.

52. SPE (Solar Proton Event)

A Solar Proton Event is when the Sun releases a burst of high-energy protons. It's like a cosmic particle shower that can affect astronauts and satellites.

53. SSBC (Solar System Boundary Crossing)

Solar System Boundary Crossing refers to spacecraft crossing the boundaries of our solar system, which is like reaching the edge of our cosmic neighbourhood.

54. SSC (Storm Sudden Commencement)

A storm's Sudden Commencement marks the quick onset of a geomagnetic storm, often caused by a shockwave from the Sun. It's like a sudden clap of thunder in space weather.

55. SSN (Sunspot Number)

The Sunspot Number counts the dark spots on the Sun's surface. These spots are like solar pimples, and more of them usually mean the Sun is more active and potentially more stormy.

56. STA (Solar Terrestrial Activity)

Solar Terrestrial Activity refers to the interactions between the Sun and Earth's environment. It's like the cosmic dance between our star and planet, influencing space weather.

57. STB (Solar Terrestrial Relations Observatory B)

The Solar Terrestrial Relations Observatory B is one of two spacecraft that give us a 3D view of the Sun.

58. SUVI (Solar Ultraviolet Imager)

The Solar Ultraviolet Imager on the GOES satellites captures images of the Sun in ultraviolet light. It's like a space telescope with UV vision, showing us the Sun's fiery outer layers.

59. SWPC (Space Weather Prediction Center)

The Space Weather Prediction Center is like a weather channel for space. These experts monitor the Sun and warn us if solar storms are approaching.

60. TEC (Total Electron Content)

Total Electron Content measures the number of electrons in a column of the Earth's atmosphere. It's like checking the airwaves' density that affects GPS signals and communications.

61. UTC (Coordinated Universal Time)

Coordinated Universal Time (UTC) is the time standard used worldwide. It's like the official clock for Earth, keeping everyone in sync no matter where they are. Most of the space forecasts online use UTC. Depending on your location, UTC must be converted to NZST or AEST.

62. VHF (Very High Frequency)

Very High-Frequency radio waves are used for TV and radio broadcasts and aircraft communication. They can travel long distances and are affected by space weather.

63. VLF (Very Low Frequency)

Very Low-Frequency waves are radio waves with long wavelengths that can travel worldwide. They're used for submarine communication and studying the ionosphere.

64. XRS (X-ray Sensor)

The X-ray Sensor on GOES satellites measures the Sun's X-ray output. It's like having X-ray vision to watch for solar flares that can affect communication and navigation systems.

65. Å (Angstrom)

An Angstrom is a unit of length used to measure the wavelengths of light, including those from the Sun. It is a tiny ruler for the very small, aiding our understanding of the Sun's spectrum.

ABOUT THE AUTHOR

Arun Chandran is a passionate explorer and community builder who lives in Melbourne with his wife. Originally from India, Arun has lived in Australia for over 12 years. His adventures have taken him to all states and territories of Australia and across the stunning landscapes of New Zealand.

Arun successfully chased Aurora in both hemispheres. His travels have spanned 59 countries, each a unique opportunity to connect with people from diverse cultures and broaden his horizons.

Arun is a committed techie who devotes his full time to his work on weekdays. However, on weekends, he dons the hat of an event organizer, orchestrating gatherings that create lasting memories. His zeal for fostering connections led him to establish the Explore Melbourne Meetup group in September 2016. Today, with a staggering 38,000 members, it proudly holds the title of Australia's largest meetup group, a testament to Arun's unwavering commitment to community and adventure.

Arun hopes to make chasing the southern lights easier for many people through this book.

ChasingAurora.com.au

www.ingramcontent.com/pod-product-compliance
Lightning Source LLC
Chambersburg PA
CBHW030546080526
44585CB00012B/273